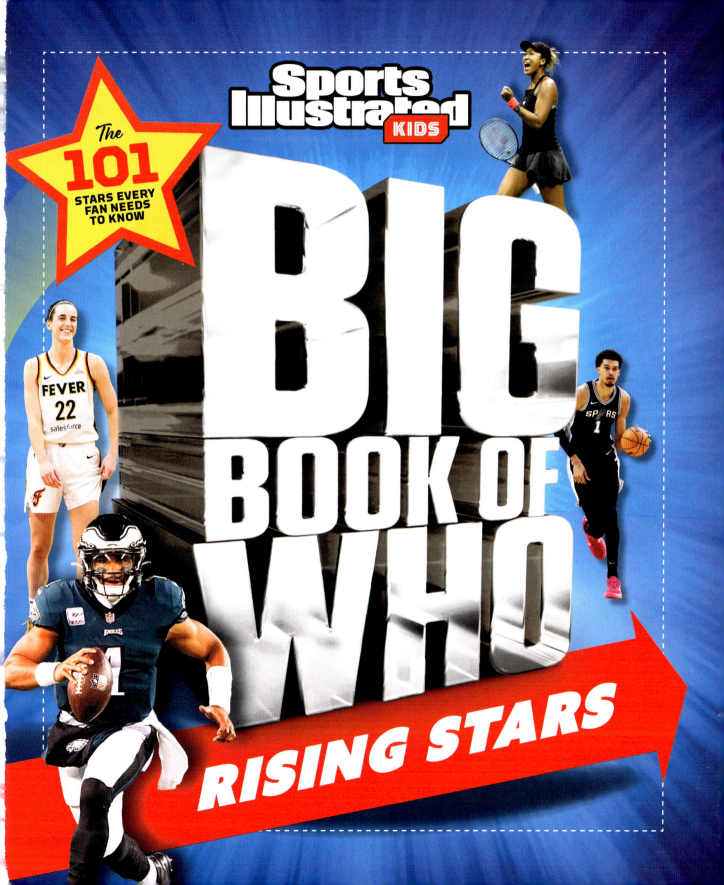

Welcome

Who is the all-time leading scorer in NCAA Division I basketball history? Who is the youngest player to lead the NFL in receiving yards? Which soccer player turns heads with the "Trin Spin"? Today's modern sports stars have proven again and again that you're never too young to make a mark or change the game. Get ready to discover a new generation of young athletes who are dominating on the football field, the basketball court, and beyond.

Copyright ©2025 ABG-SI LLC. Used under license.

No part of this publication may be reproduced, stored in a retrieval system, or transmitted in any form by any means, electronic, mechanical, photocopying, or otherwise, without the prior written permission of the publisher, Triumph Books LLC, 814 North Franklin Street, Chicago, Illinois 60610.

Library of Congress Cataloging-in-Publication Data available upon request.

This book is available in quantity at special discounts for your group or organization.
For further information, contact:

Triumph Books LLC
814 North Franklin Street
Chicago, Illinois 60610
(312) 337-0747
www.triumphbooks.com

Cover design by Preston Pisellini
Text by Adam Motin

Printed in China

978-1-63727-536-8

Contents

Next Generation	4
Phenoms	30
Record Breakers	54
Trailblazers	78
Trendsetters	104
PLAYER INDEX	126
PHOTO CREDITS	128

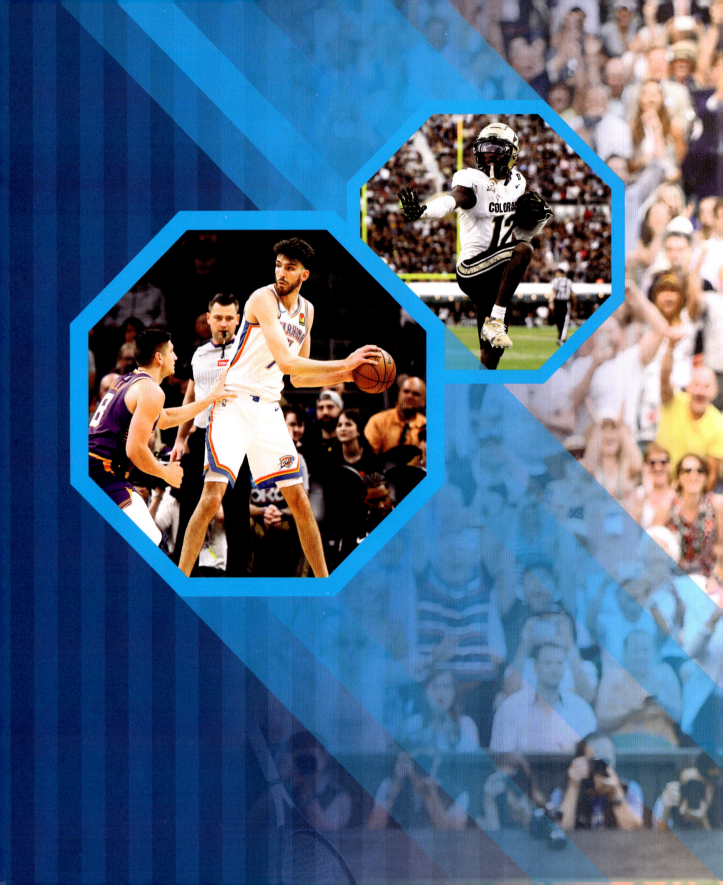

Who was the first Orlando Magic teenager to post 30 points and 15 rebounds in an NBA game?

The Orlando Magic surprised many observers when they selected **Paolo Banchero** with the first pick in the 2022 NBA Draft. It wasn't because Banchero was unworthy—he'd averaged 17.2 points per game in his only season at Duke University—but rather that he wasn't seen as a can't-miss prospect. But Banchero made believers out of everyone from the start, scoring 27 points in his regular-season debut. That November, he totaled 33 points and 16 rebounds in a game against the Sacramento Kings, becoming the youngest Magic player to put up at least 30 points and 15 rebounds in a game. Banchero was named the league's Rookie of the Year, and the following season earned his first All-Star Game selection. In his first playoff appearance, he scored 24 points, then posted a playoff career-high 39 points in a Game 5 loss to the Cleveland Cavaliers.

★ DID YOU KNOW? ★

Banchero's mother, Rhonda, left the University of Washington as that program's all-time scoring leader. She was a third-round selection in the 2000 WNBA Draft. His father played football at Washington and is of Italian descent, making Banchero eligible to play for either Italy or the U.S. in international competitions.

NEXT GENERATION

Who was the youngest USWNT player to score multiple goals in her World Cup debut?

On their way to a three-on-three soccer game, five-year-old **Sophia Wilson** says she told her father she would score 10 goals in the match. She did. It was an early sign that Wilson was both supremely talented and very confident. Those traits followed her to Stanford University and then to the NWSL, where she was the first teenager ever selected in that league's draft, by the Portland Thorns FC. In her second full professional season, Wilson set the club's single-season record for goals, won the NWSL MVP award, and was named MVP of the NWSL championship game. In her first international game for the USWNT, she scored two goals in a game against Vietnam in the 2023 World Cup, becoming the youngest American woman to score twice in her World Cup debut. Though the U.S. was eliminated from that tournament, Wilson and her teammates bounced back in 2024, winning the CONCACAF Gold Cup and the gold medal at the 2024 Paris Olympics.

★ DID YOU KNOW? ★
Sophia's father played college basketball at Wyoming, and she and her sisters, Savannah and Gabrielle, also played the game growing up. Savannah graduated from the University of Northern Colorado as that school's all-time leading scorer.

★ FAST FACT ★
Only two other Gonzaga Bulldogs have been selected in the top five of an NBA draft: Jalen Suggs (No. 5, 2021) and Adam Morrison (No. 3, 2006).

Who is the highest-drafted player in Gonzaga men's basketball history?

Heading into the 2022 NBA Draft, teams at the top had their choice of big men, including Duke's Paolo Banchero and Auburn's Jabari Smith Jr. But with the second overall pick, the Oklahoma City Thunder selected 7'1" Chet Holmgren from Gonzaga, and they are glad they did. After sitting out his entire rookie season with a foot injury, Holmgren broke out in 2023–24, averaging 16.5 points and 7.9 rebounds per game as the Thunder claimed the top seed in the Western Conference. Season highlights included scoring a career-high 36 points in an overtime win against the Golden State Warriors in November, and scoring 26 points against the New Orleans Pelicans in a first-round playoff game.

NEXT GENERATION

Who is the most recent player to win five straight LPGA events?

Golf is a difficult sport to master; even the best players in the world can have a bad day on the course. That's why what **Nelly Korda** accomplished in 2024 was so remarkable. Beginning with a victory at the LPGA Drive On Championship in January, Korda won five straight tournaments, a feat matched in history only by golfing legends Nancy Lopez (1978) and Annika Sörenstam (2004–2005). Winning is nothing new for Korda; she won the Women's PGA Championship in 2021, the Chevron Championship in 2024, and has been ranked No. 1 in the world. She also won the gold medal in women's golf at the 2020 Summer Olympics in Tokyo.

★ **DID YOU KNOW?** ★

Korda's older sister, Jessica, also plays on the LPGA Tour, but the rest of their family excelled at a different sport. Their parents, Petr Korda and Regina Rajchrtová, were both professional tennis players, and their brother, Sebastian, has been ranked as high as No. 15 in the world.

★ **FAST FACT** ★
Gu scored a 1580 out of 1600 on her SAT exam and gained early admittance to Stanford University, in 2020.

NEXT GENERATION

★ DID YOU KNOW? ★

Gu decided to represent China at the Olympics because while her sport is already established in the United States, she wanted to show kids in China that anything was possible. "It was remarkable hearing from kids who are 11, 12 years old, telling me I changed the course of their lives," she said. "That's a very profound thought for a tween to be having, and it's something I don't take lightly."

Who was the first freestyle skier to win three medals at a single Winter Olympics?

Freestyle skier **Eileen Gu** had an unlikely start to her athletic journey. Raised by a single mother who had emigrated from China, Gu grew up in San Francisco, perhaps not the first place that comes to mind when you think of winter sports. But Gu began skiing at the age of three, won her first national championship at nine, and has been making history ever since. At the 2021 Winter X Games, Gu won two gold medals and a bronze, becoming the first rookie to medal in three events. She repeated that feat at the 2022 Winter Olympics, where she became the youngest gold medalist in freestyle skiing, winning the big air event, and won a second gold medal in the freeski halfpipe and a silver in the slopestyle.

STAR POWER

57.8%

Boston's field-goal percentage in 2023–24. She became the first rookie to ever lead the league in that category.

Who was the unanimous WNBA Rookie of the Year in 2023–24?

Though her teammate Caitlin Clark might get all the headlines, Indiana Fever forward **Aliyah Boston** is equally deserving of the spotlight. A three-time Massachusetts Player of the Year in high school, Boston went to college at the University of South Carolina, where she became the first freshman to ever record a triple-double in her debut. As a junior, she collected 11 points and 16 rebounds in her team's championship game victory against the University of Connecticut; it was her 30th double-double of the season. Indiana made Boston the first pick of the 2023 WNBA Draft, and she paid immediate dividends, winning three Rookie of the Month awards and becoming just the eighth rookie in league history to start in the All-Star Game. At the end of the season, Boston was unanimously named WNBA Rookie of the Year.

NEXT GENERATION

Who set a speed climbing world record at the 2024 Summer Olympics?

If you are interested in watching speed climbing—a discipline where competitors scale a standardized climbing wall as quickly as possible—you better be there on time. Elite athletes reach the top of the 49-foot wall in around five seconds, and no one did it faster in 2024 than **Sam Watson**. Born and raised in Texas before his family moved to Utah, Watson began climbing when he was five years old, and by age 18 had set and then broken his own world record at the World Cup in Wujiang, in 2024. Later that year he repeated the feat at the 2024 Summer Olympics, setting a new world record at 4.75 and then lowering it further, to 4.74. Watson has placed first at three World Cup events and won a bronze medal at the 2024 Games in Paris.

★ **DID YOU KNOW?** ★

Watson enjoys playing chess, and posted on Instagram looking for someone to play with at the Olympic Village in Paris. "[Chess is] similar to climbing, you're just trying to improve and every move leads to a position," he told Olympics.com.

STAR POWER
37–0
Elor's international record between 2019 and the start of the 2024 Summer Olympics.

Who was the youngest American to win an Olympic gold medal in wrestling?

When **Amit Elor** began wrestling as a child, her mother says coaches would tell her, "Go easy on the boys." Elor hasn't taken it easy on many competitors in the years since, dominating most of the freestyle wrestling events she's entered. As a high school freshman, she went 36–0 and won the California state championship after pinning her final opponent in 20 seconds. Elor was an eight-time gold medalist at World Championships, which included a victory at the 2022 World Wrestling Championships that made her the youngest American world champion in history. She complemented that feat at the 2024 Olympic Games in Paris, where she won in women's freestyle wrestling 68kg, becoming the youngest gold medal winner in American wrestling history, at the age of 20.

★ FAST FACT ★
Born in California to Israeli parents, Elor only spoke Hebrew until she began preschool.

NEXT GENERATION

Which tight end set a single-season rookie record for most receptions and receiving yards?

The NFL's next great tight end may have arrived in 2024 with the debut of Los Angeles Raider **Brock Bowers**. A three-time All-American and two-time national champion at the University of Georgia, the Raiders made Bowers the 13th selection in the 2024 NFL Draft. He recorded six receptions for 58 yards in the season opener and never let up, playing in all 17 games and finishing the season with 112 catches for 1,194 yards, totals that led all NFL tight ends. Bowers set a new mark for most receiving yards by a rookie tight end, a record that had stood for more than 60 years. He also broke the record for most receptions by a rookie of any position, set in 2023 by Rams wide receiver Puka Nacua. Bowers was named First-Team All-Pro, the first tight end to be so honored since Jeremy Shockey, in 2002.

STAR POWER

1,076

Receiving yards by Mike Ditka in 1961, the most by a rookie tight end until Bowers' 1,194 in 2024.

★ **DID YOU KNOW?** ★
Jackson's brother, Jaison, is also a highly regarded prospect. The Cleveland Guardians signed him to $1.2 million contract in 2022.

Who is the youngest MLB player to post a 20-20 season?

The 2024 season was a tale of two halves for Milwaukee Brewers outfielder **Jackson Chourio**. Named the game's top prospect by Baseball America in 2023, Chourio played in the All-Star Futures Game that year and had already signed an eight-year contract with Milwaukee before making his big-league debut. After starting on Opening Day, Chourio struggled at the plate, hitting just .210 as late as June. But he soon turned things around, and in September hit his 20th home run of the season in a game against the San Francisco Giants, becoming the youngest player in MLB history (at 20 years, 185 days) to hit at least 20 homers and steal at least 20 bases in a season. In the 2024 NL Wild Card Series, against the New York Mets, Chourio hit two game-tying home runs in Game 2. He was the first player to achieve such a feat since Babe Ruth in the 1928 World Series.

NEXT GENERATION

Who set an NHL single-season rookie record for total ice time?

It has often been said that the best ability is availability; in other words, sometimes showing up for every game is just as important as how you play. No NHL rookie exemplified that better than Minnesota Wild defenseman **Brock Faber** in 2023–24. Originally drafted by the Los Angeles Kings in 2020, Faber was traded to Minnesota in 2022 and appeared in all 82 games for the Wild in 2023–24. He tied Connor Bedard for the most assists among rookies (39) and set franchise rookie records for assists, points, blocked shots, and ice time. Faber's total time on ice, 2,047:53, was the most by a rookie since the NHL began recording the statistic in 1997–98. He was also a finalist for the Calder Trophy and was named to the NHL All-Rookie Team.

Who holds the record for most passing yards in a game by a rookie?

In 2023, the Houston Texans went looking for a new franchise quarterback and believed they'd found their man with the second overall pick in the draft. A two-time Heisman Trophy finalist at Ohio State, **C.J. Stroud** wasted little time turning the rest of the NFL into believers. Stroud started 15 games for the Texans and set a slew of rookie records along the way. In Week 9 against Tampa Bay, he passed for 470 yards, the most ever by a rookie in a single game, breaking the mark previously held by Andrew Luck. But Stroud was far from done. By the end of the season, he'd become just the fifth quarterback in history to pass for over 4,000 yards in their rookie season, and just the third player to lead the league in passing yards per game and touchdown/interception ratio in the same season. In his playoff debut against the Cleveland Browns, Stroud became the youngest quarterback to win a playoff game in NFL history.

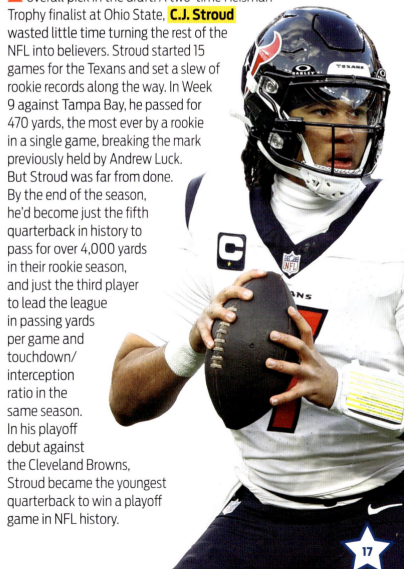

17

STAR POWER

28.5

Hutchinson's career sack total over his first three NFL seasons.

Who was the first Detroit Lion to collect a sack in five consecutive games?

As a senior at the University of Michigan, defensive lineman **Aidan Hutchinson** won the Ted Hendricks and Lombardi awards for his excellence in rushing the passer. So when the Detroit Lions selected him with the second pick of the 2022 NFL Draft, they knew he was capable of rewriting the franchise's record book. Hutchinson delivered, finishing his rookie season with 9.5 sacks—three of them in a record-setting performance in Week 2—52 total tackles, three interceptions, and two fumble recoveries. In 2023, he upped his sack total to 11.5 and was named to his first Pro Bowl. He continued to dominate in 2024, before an injury ended his season: one week after setting a franchise record for the most sacks (10.5) in any four-game stretch, Hutchinson recorded a sack for the fifth consecutive regular-season game, the longest streak in Lions history.

★ DID YOU KNOW? ★

Brink started her own basketball camp in Oregon, Next22, focusing on girls in fifth through eighth grade. "My main message was that you don't have to become a pro, you don't have to be the best—it's not all about that," she told SI. "It's about making connections. It's about leadership skills. It's about connecting within your community. And the biggest thing for me is [fostering] self-confidence and self-esteem—because that's what sports do for girls."

Which Stanford basketball player was the Pac-12 POY and DPOY in 2023–24?

For someone who wasn't that interested in playing basketball as a kid, **Cameron Brink** has already had an incredible career on the court. The daughter of two former college basketball players, Brink received a scholarship offer from Stanford University as a seventh-grader and began playing for the Cardinal in 2020. As a freshman, she helped her team win the national championship, scoring 10 points and blocking three shots in the title game against Arizona, and was named to the Pac-12 All-Freshman Team. The next season, Stanford got back to the Elite Eight and Brink was named the conference's Player of the Year and Defensive Player of the Year, a feat she repeated as a senior in 2023–24. She left Stanford as the school's all-time leader in blocked shots, and was drafted second overall by the Los Angeles Sparks in the 2024 WNBA Draft.

Who led the NBA in assists in 2023–24?

When the Indiana Pacers traded their All-Star center, Domantas Sabonis, to the Sacramento Kings in a deal to acquire **Tyrese Haliburton**, they were counting on the former Iowa State point guard's continued development. Their faith has been rewarded, as Haliburton has been named to two All-Star teams and an All-NBA Third Team during his time in Indiana. Haliburton had been named to the All-Rookie First Team as a King, but Sacramento decided his fit alongside fellow All-Star De'Aaron Fox was less than ideal. The Kings' loss has been the Pacers' gain. While his career scoring average is a respectable 17.2 points per game entering the 2024–25 season, setting up his teammates is where Haliburton truly shines: he is tied for the franchise record for most assists in one game (23) and owns the mark for most assists in a season (752). His 10.9 assists per game led the entire NBA in 2023–24.

★ DID YOU KNOW? ★

Haliburton is a big fan of WWE and has appeared on their televised programming on multiple occasions. The company even released a branded "Haliburton 3:17" T-shirt, a reference to both "Stone Cold" Steve Austin and the Indianapolis area code.

NEXT GENERATION

STAR POWER

7

Number of games during 2023 season in which Lamb caught at least 11 passes, an NFL record.

★ **DID YOU KNOW?** ★

As a kid, Lamb spent time on his father's ranch in Louisiana, where he developed a love for horses and riding four-wheelers.

Who led the NFL in receptions in 2023?

During his first three seasons at the University of Oklahoma, **CeeDee Lamb** caught passes from quarterbacks who either won the Heisman Trophy (Baker Mayfield, Kyler Murray) or finished second in the voting (Jalen Hurts). While that's an enviable environment for any receiver, it could also be said he did as much for his quarterbacks as they did for him, finishing his collegiate career with 3,292 receiving yards and 32 touchdowns. Lamb has been similarly productive for the Dallas Cowboys after they selected him with the 17th pick in the 2020 NFL Draft. He finished second among rookies in receiving yards, then went over 1,000 yards in each of the next three seasons. Lamb truly broke out in 2023, amassing 1,749 yards and 135 receptions, the most in the NFL. Both numbers set franchise records for Dallas receivers.

★ **FAST FACT** ★

CeeDee's full name is Cedarian DeLeon Lamb.

21

★ **DID YOU KNOW?** ★

In 2023, Rodriguez played in a match between Nebraska and the University of Nebraska–Omaha in front of 92,003 people at Memorial Stadium, the largest crowd for a women's sporting event in U.S. history.

Which volleyball star had a day named in her honor in Sterling, Illinois?

The University of Nebraska's women's volleyball team is the sport's gold standard; no program has won more matches or spent more weeks ranked No. 1. It takes something special for a player to stand out amongst the other Cornhuskers, but that's exactly what Lexi Rodriguez brought with her to Lincoln. In 2021, Rodriguez was the first libero—the defensive specialist who wears a different jersey from their teammates—ever named AVCA National Freshman of the Year. She was a four-time All-American, a three-time Big Ten Defensive Player of the Year, and set the school's career record for digs. In high school, she led her team to two state titles and was the 2019–20 Illinois Volleyball Gatorade Player of the Year. Her hometown of Sterling declared December 21, 2021, as Lexi Rodriguez Day.

NEXT GENERATION

★ FAST FACT ★
Musah is fluent in multiple languages, including English, Spanish, Italian, Dagbani, and Hausa.

Which USMNT player was also eligible to play for England, Ghana, and Italy?

Midfielder **Yunus Musah** is a unique figure both on and off the pitch. By the age of nine, he had displayed enough promise to join Arsenal's Academy in London. When he was 16, he signed a professional contract with Valencia in Spain, where his combination of speed and athleticism led to him becoming the youngest foreign-born footballer to ever play for Valencia's senior team. Musah's personal background also makes him stand out: he was born in New York City to Ghanian parents, but the family soon moved to the northern Italian town of Castelfranco Veneto before relocating again to London. That means Musah was eligible to play internationally for four different countries; in fact, he did play for England 32 times at the youth level. However, since 2020 Musah has been a member of the USMNT.

Who is the youngest player to be named USA Basketball's Male Athlete of the Year?

Since 1980, USA Basketball has honored its top male and female players on an annual basis, based on that year's international competition. On the men's side, the list of past winners is a who's who of basketball royalty, including LeBron James, Kevin Durant, Shaquille O'Neal, and Michael Jordan. Joining that illustrious company in 2022 was **Cooper Flagg**, the high school phenom from Maine. The announcement of his selection was made on his 16th birthday, making him the youngest player to ever win the award. Flagg had shined at the FIBA Men's U17 World Cup that summer, as Team USA went 7–0 and won the gold medal. Despite being just 15 at the time, Flagg averaged 9.3 points and 10 rebounds per game, pulling down 17 boards in the final game, a men's U17 record. In July 2024, Flagg played for the USA Select Team that nearly beat eventual 2024 Olympic champion Team USA in a scrimmage.

★ FAST FACT ★

As a freshman at Nokomis Regional High School in Maine, Flagg averaged 20.5 points, 10 rebounds, 6.2 assists, 3.7 steals, and 3.7 blocks, and led his team to the school's first state basketball championship.

NEXT GENERATION

★ **DID YOU KNOW?** ★
Gauff grew up idolizing Serena and Venus Williams, and made that clear to Venus after defeating her at Wimbledon in 2019. "I was just telling her thank you for everything she's done for the sport," Gauff said. "She's been an inspiration for many people. I was just really telling her thank you."

Who is the youngest player to qualify for the main draw at Wimbledon in the Open Era?

When the Wimbledon Championships began in 2019, American phenom Coco Gauff was only a few months past her 15th birthday. Nevertheless, after winning four matches during a qualifying tournament prior to the event, Gauff made history by becoming the youngest qualifier to reach the main draw in the Open Era. Her run didn't stop there: she upset five-time champion Venus Williams in her opening match, then advanced to the fourth round before losing to eventual Wimbledon winner Simona Halep. Gauff later won the U.S. Open, in 2023, and has been ranked as high as No. 2 in the world.

STAR POWER

4

Number of freshmen who have won the Hobey Baker Award: Celebrini, Paul Kariya (1993), Jack Eichel (2015), and Adam Fantilli (2023).

Who is the youngest hockey player to win the Hobey Baker Award?

Growing up in Vancouver, **Macklin Celebrini** dreamed of one day playing hockey in Rogers Arena, home of the NHL's Canucks. That dream came true in 2024, though Celebrini wasn't wearing a Canucks sweater; he was a member of the visiting San Jose Sharks, who had made him the top overall pick in the 2024 NHL Draft. Celebrini played for the Chicago Steel of the United States Hockey League in 2022–23, recording 86 points during the season, a total that led the USHL and was the most ever by an under-17 player in league history. The following year, he played alongside his brother at Boston University, where he registered 32 goals and 64 points in just 38 games. He also won the Hobey Baker Award, given annually to the NCAA's top player. At 17 years old, Celebrini became the youngest player to win the award. Months later, he scored a goal and collected an assist in his NHL debut.

NEXT GENERATION

★ FAST FACT ★

Merrill became the youngest Padre to ever homer in the postseason after going yard in the 2024 NLDS against the Los Angeles Dodgers. Only three center fielders have ever homered in the playoffs at a younger age: Bryce Harper, Andruw Jones, and Mickey Mantle.

Who was the first San Diego Padres rookie named to the All-Star Game?

As one of the top prospects in all of baseball, **Jackson Merrill** probably thought he would spend his major league career at shortstop, the position he'd played most of his life. But when the 2024 season began, Merrill found himself a new home in center field. The switch might have bothered most players, but it didn't affect Merrill; in his first season, he batted .292, hit 24 home runs, and drove in 90 runs, all while playing a demanding position. His performance earned him a spot in the All-Star Game that July, becoming the first Padres rookie ever to be so honored. At the end of the season, Merrill was named a recipient of the NL Silver Slugger Award.

27

★ **DID YOU KNOW?** ★

Hunter majored in anthropology at Colorado. "I really enjoy learning about different cultures and how they interact with one another," Hunter told USA TODAY Sports. "Being able to learn about these cultures and skills is incredibly beneficial to me even when playing football. I have the opportunity to learn the importance of accepting and interacting with other people and playing with other people despite their cultural or ethnic makeup."

Who won the Heisman Trophy in 2024?

Deion Sanders was famous for being multitalented; for example, playing cornerback and returning punts in the NFL, then playing center field in Major League Baseball. So it's no surprise that college football's newest two-way star, Travis Hunter, jumped at the chance to play for Sanders, first at Jackson State and then at the University of Colorado. A standout at both cornerback and wide receiver, Hunter filled up the highlight reels; in his first game as a Buffalo, in 2023, he had 11 receptions for 119 yards, as well as three tackles and an interception, as Colorado upset TCU. In 2024, he finished the regular season playing almost 1,400 snaps from scrimmage on offense and defense, 382 more than any other player in the country. He was rewarded with the Heisman Trophy, becoming only the second defensive player to win the award. (Michigan's Charles Woodson in 1997 is the other.) He is also the first player in history to win both the Chuck Bednarik Award, as the nation's top defensive player, and the Fred Biletnikoff Award, as the nation's top wide receiver.

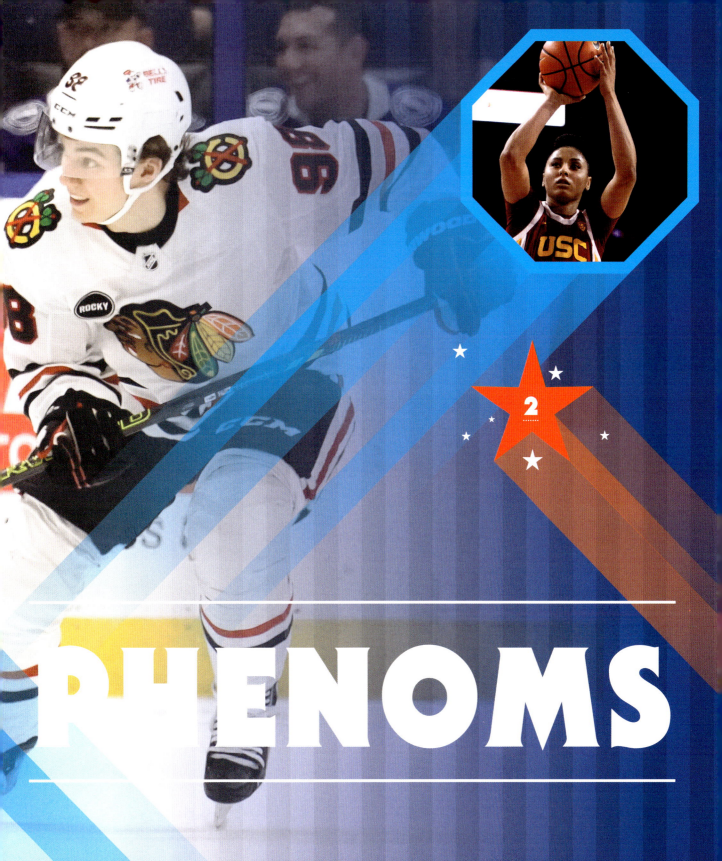

PHENOMS

STAR POWER
14%
The Spurs' probability of getting the No. 1 pick—along with the franchise-altering Wembanyama—in the 2023 NBA Draft.

Who is the youngest Spur to record at least 40 points and 20 rebounds in an NBA game?

Not since LeBron James had there been a hotter NBA prospect than **Victor Wembanyama**. The 7'3" teenager from France had the skills of a guard in a giant's body, and in 2022–23 became the youngest player to lead France's top league in scoring, rebounds, and blocks, in addition to winning its awards for MVP and best defensive player. After the San Antonio Spurs selected him first overall in the 2023 NBA Draft, the 19-year-old Wembanyama did not disappoint in his rookie season. In addition to filling the highlight reels on a nightly basis, Wembanyama became the first player in NBA history to record 1,500 points, 700 rebounds, 250 assists, 250 blocks, and 100 three-pointers in a single season; nearly recorded a quadruple-double in a game against Denver; led the league in blocks; and was the first rookie ever named to the All-Defensive First Team. On March 29, 2024, against the New York Knicks, he became the youngest player to score 40 points and snatch 20 rebounds in San Antonio history.

★ FAST FACT ★
A jersey Wembanyama wore in his NBA debut was sold at Sotheby's in 2023 for $762,000, the most ever for a jersey of its kind.

PHENOMS

★ DID YOU KNOW? ★

Wembanyama is from an athletic family: his 6'6" father is a former track and field athlete, while his 6'3" mother is a former basketball player and now coach. His sister, Eve, won gold at the FIBA U16 European basketball championships in 2017, and his younger brother Oscar is playing for Strasbourg's U21 team.

Who was the first overall pick of the 2024 PWHL Draft?

It's hard to imagine a player entering the PWHL with more gold on her résumé than **Sarah Fillier**. A native of Ontario, Canada, Fillier played hockey at Princeton University, and led the NCAA in points per game as a freshman and goals per game as a senior. She was a three-time finalist for the Patty Kazmaier Award, given each year to the nation's top player. Fillier has truly shone in international competition, where she has helped Canada win three world championships (2021, 2022, 2024) and was named MVP of the tournament in 2023. She also led Canada to a gold medal at the 2022 Winter Olympics in Beijing, scoring eight goals, including a hat trick against Sweden. New York hoped Fillier would bring her winning ways with her after selecting her with the first pick of the 2024 PWHL Draft.

★ **FAST FACT** ★
Fillier graduated from Princeton University with a degree in psychology.

PHENOMS

★ FAST FACT ★
Nacua's brother Kai played safety for the San Francisco 49ers, the Cleveland Browns, and the New York Jets. Their brother Samson was signed by the New Orleans Saints as a receiver in 2024.

Which L.A. Rams receiver had arguably the greatest rookie season in NFL history?

If teams had known how effective receiver **Puka Nacua** was going to be, he never would've lasted until the 177th pick of the 2023 NFL Draft. After a solid college career at Washington and BYU, the Los Angeles Rams selected him in the fifth round, likely hoping he could add to the team's depth at wide receiver. What they got instead was a receiver who rewrote the rookie record book. In his first game, he caught 10 passes for 119 yards, then hauled in 15 passes in Week 2 to break the record for catches by a rookie in a single game. By Week 13, he'd already passed 1,000 yards for the season, and he finished the regular season with 105 receptions for 1,486 yards to set new rookie records in both categories. In his first career playoff game, Nacua caught nine passes for 181 yards in a wild card game against the Detroit Lions to break the single-game playoff record for receiving yards by a rookie.

★ DID YOU KNOW? ★
Nacua's first name is actually Makea. "Puka" means chubby in Samoan, and was Nacua's nickname because of his size as a baby.

35

PHENOMS

STAR POWER

5

Rodman's ranking among the world's 100 best female soccer players in 2024, according to *The Guardian*.

Which soccer player turns heads with the "Trin Spin"?

When your dad is NBA Hall of Famer Dennis Rodman, making your own name in the world of sports might seem like a daunting task. But it hasn't been a problem for soccer star **Trinity Rodman**. When she was selected second overall in the 2021 NWSL Draft by the Washington Spirit, she was the youngest draftee in NWSL history at the time. She helped the Spirit win the NWSL championship that season, and was named Rookie of the Year and to the NWSL Best XI. Rodman has also represented the United States at CONCACAF, the World Cup, and the 2024 Summer Olympics in Paris, where her team won the gold medal. She's also faked out multiple defenders with the "Trin Spin," a fancy bit of footwork that leaves Rodman and the ball going one way and her opponent facing the other.

★ **DID YOU KNOW?** ★

In 2022, Rodman worked with adidas to publish *Wake Up and Kick It*, an inspirational book for kids from all walks of life. "Paving my own, unique path has never been easy, but I have always had unmatchable work ethic, been able to ignore outside noise and wake up and tackle each day as it comes," Rodman said. "I'm excited for this book to inspire the next generation to go out and achieve their goals and dreams, proving that nothing is out of reach if you are willing to work for it."

STAR POWER

160

Number of games De La Cruz played in 2024, third-most in the NL.

Who led MLB in steals in 2024?

The most exciting thing about Cincinnati Reds shortstop **Elly De La Cruz** is not that he led his team in home runs, triples, and doubles in 2024; it's that he has so much room to improve. When the infielder made his major league debut in 2023, his physical gifts were immediately on display: he broke the Statcast record for fastest infield assist (97.9 mph); his maximum exit velocity was in the 98th percentile; and he averaged 30.5 feet per second in terms of sprint speed. In his first full season in the big leagues, De La Cruz became the first player since Ichiro Suzuki in 2012 to record four hits and four stolen bases in a single game, in May against the Los Angeles Dodgers. He set a Reds record for most stolen bases (45) before the All-Star break and was subsequently named to the NL team. At season's end, De La Cruz led the majors with 67 stolen bases; he was also the first shortstop in history to hit at least 20 home runs and steal at least 60 bases in a season.

PHENOMS

Who is the youngest woman to compete in a World Surf League event?

The word prodigy is often used to describe 22-year-old surfer **Caroline Marks**. It's an apt description: she began surfing at the age of eight, won a top amateur competition when she was 11, and at 15 became the youngest man or woman to qualify for the World Surf League's Championship Tour. She was the Tour's Rookie of the Year in 2018, finished second in 2019, then took home the women's championship in 2023 at the age of 21. When she's not surfing on the pro circuit, she's represented the United States at the Olympics, just missing out on the bronze medal at the 2020 Games in Tokyo, then returning to win the gold at the 2024 Games in Paris. She is the second American women's surfing gold medalist; in the first appearance of the event in 2020, Carissa Moore took home the gold.

★ **FAST FACT** ★
Before taking up surfing, Marks competed in barrel racing, a rodeo event on horseback.

★ **FAST FACT** ★

Bedard was the second No. 1 pick in Blackhawks history. The franchise selected winger Patrick Kane with the No. 1 pick in 2007.

Who was the 2023–24 NHL Rookie of the Year?

When the Chicago Blackhawks were awarded the first pick in the 2023 NHL Draft, there was no doubt who they would select: **Connor Bedard**, a center from British Columbia who entered the league with more hype than perhaps any prospect in history. Bedard had been projected as hockey's Next Big Thing for years, having already been named the Rookie of the Year and MVP in the Western Hockey League, as well as winning championships with the Canadian national under-18 team in 2021 and with the Canadian national junior team in 2022 and 2023. (He set several scoring records in the 2023 tournament and was named the MVP.) During his first NHL season, Bedard suffered a broken jaw in January that kept him out of 14 games. Nevertheless, he led all rookies in goals (22) and points (61) and won the Calder Trophy as the league's top newcomer.

★ **DID YOU KNOW?** ★

Bedard says Sidney Crosby was his childhood idol, and the two faced off in Bedard's NHL debut. "[I was] just trying to win [the draw], and I failed miserably," he told ESPN. "But it was pretty cool. He's a childhood hero of mine, like I've mentioned. It was a lot of fun."

PHENOMS

STAR POWER

23

Points Bedard scored in just seven games during the 2023 World Junior Ice Hockey Championships.

★ DID YOU KNOW? ★

Tennis isn't the only game Alcaraz likes to play. "I love chess. Having to concentrate, to play against someone else, strategy—having to think ahead. I think all of that is very similar to the tennis court," he told *Vogue*. "You have to intuit where the other player is going to send the ball, you have to move ahead of time, and try to do something that will make him uncomfortable. So I play it a lot."

Who is the youngest player to reach No. 1 in the ATP rankings?

Men's professional tennis is often dominated by a few era-defining players; think Roger Federer, Rafael Nadal, and Novak Djokovic. The next competitor to join that list might be **Carlos Alcaraz** from Spain. Since joining the ATP tour in 2020 at the age of 16, Alcaraz has been on a tear, winning the U.S. Open (2022), Wimbledon (2023, 2024), and the French Open (2024), meaning only a win at the Australian Open stands between him and completion of a Grand Slam. After his victory at the U.S. Open, he became the youngest player to be ranked No. 1 in ATP history, at 19 years and four months. With speed that compares to his fellow countryman Nadal and court coverage that rivals Djokovic, Alcaraz will likely spend plenty of weeks atop the rankings.

PHENOMS

STAR POWER

4

Number of players selected first overall in both the PLL and NLL drafts (O'Neill, Kevin Crowley [2012], Lyle Thompson [2015], and Jeff Teat [2020]).

Which lacrosse player was the first pick in two different drafts in 2024?

Being the first overall selection in a professional sports league's draft is the childhood dream of many aspiring athletes. But how about doing it *twice*? That is the rare feat lacrosse star **Brennan O'Neill** achieved in 2024. As a high school player in New York, O'Neill was named the USA Lacrosse National Player of the Year in 2019 after scoring seven goals in his state championship game. At Duke University, he led the team in goals as a freshman and a sophomore, led the nation in points as a junior, and ranks third in Duke history and fifth in NCAA history in career goals. On the international stage, he led the U.S. team to the gold medal at the U21 World Championship, then won gold again with the Men's National Team at the 2023 World Men's Lacrosse Championship, where he was named the tournament's Most Outstanding Player. It's no wonder that in 2024 he was the first pick of both the Premier Lacrosse League draft and the National Lacrosse League draft, by the Denver Outlaws and Philadelphia Wings, respectively.

43

★ **DID YOU KNOW?** ★
Skenes is dating gymnast and social media star Livvy Dunne. The two met at LSU, where Skenes' best friend was dating Dunne's roommate.

PHENOMS

STAR POWER
17
Number of 100-mph fastballs Skenes threw against the Cubs in his first start.

Who was the first No. 1 overall draft pick to start an MLB All-Star Game as a rookie?

In 2024, Pittsburgh Pirates right-hander **Paul Skenes** had a rookie season for the ages. After winning the 2023 Men's College World Series with LSU and being named the tournament's Most Outstanding Player, the flame-throwing Skenes was selected with the first pick in the draft and was fast-tracked to the majors. By May 2024, he was ready for his big-league debut, where he struck out seven Chicago Cubs in four innings. By midseason, Skenes' ERA stood at 1.90, and he'd set a Pirates record by striking out at least seven batters in eight consecutive starts. Those numbers led to him not only being named to the All-Star Game but earned him the starting spot, an honor given to only four other rookies in history. He finished the season with an 11–3 record, a 1.96 ERA, and 170 strikeouts over 133 innings pitched, and was named the NL Rookie of the Year.

Who is the youngest player to make 600 career three-pointers in the NBA?

In the 2020 NBA Draft, the Minnesota Timberwolves selected dynamic shooting guard **Anthony Edwards** with the first overall pick. During his single season at the University of Georgia, Edwards was the nation's top scoring freshman (19.1) and was also one of five finalists for the Jerry West Award, given to the country's best shooting guard. Once he got to Minnesota, his powerful drives to the basket and improving jumper made an instant impact, and he finished second in the Rookie of the Year race. In the 2023–24 season opener against Toronto, Edwards hit a three in the first quarter to become the youngest player ever to make 600 career threes, at the age of 22. Edwards led Minnesota to its first playoff series victory in 20 years at the end of that season, a run that ended in the Western Conference Finals against Dallas.

★ **DID YOU KNOW?** ★

Edwards made his acting debut in the film *Hustle*, starring Adam Sandler, in 2022. The guard plays a competitor and antagonist of the character played by Juancho Hernangómez, himself a former member of the Timberwolves.

PHENOMS

Who is the youngest Olympic medalist in Great Britain's history?

To call **Sky Brown** a skateboarding phenom understates what the 17-year-old has already accomplished. When she was just eight years old, she became the youngest skater to compete in the Vans US Open. Two years later, Brown turned pro, becoming the youngest professional skateboarder in the world. She then represented Great Britain at the delayed 2020 Tokyo Olympics, the first time skateboarding was included in the Games. Brown took home the bronze medal in the women's park skateboarding event; at just 13 years and 28 days, she is Great Britain's youngest medal winner. She won bronze again in the same event at the 2024 Olympics in Paris.

★ FAST FACT ★
Brown's dad is English, but moved to the United States when he was a teenager. He and Sky's mom, Mieko, met in Japan, which is where their daughter was born. Sky spends half the school year in Japan and the other half in the U.S.

47

★ DID YOU KNOW? ★

Watkins was named the 2020 Sports Kid of the Year by *Sports Illustrated Kids*, not just for her play on the court, but for her desire to influence and motivate others. "I want to inspire people, no matter where they come from, to believe in yourself and always push to be great," Watkins said.

Who owns the single-season freshman scoring record in NCAA women's basketball history?

A native of Los Angeles and the No. 1 recruit in her high school class, **JuJu Watkins** chose to play college basketball for the USC Trojans starting in 2023–24. She put together a historic season, breaking the single-season freshmen scoring record with 920 points, a total that shattered a mark that had stood for 40 years. Watkins averaged 27 points per game while scoring from everywhere on the floor: she shot 40.1 percent from the field and 85.2 percent from the free throw line. Watkins scored 30 or more points in 14 games; her highest-scoring game came against Stanford, when she poured in 51 points in a winning effort. Far from a one-dimensional player, she earned a Pac-12 All-Defensive Team honorable mention at the end of the regular season, and was predictably named Pac-12 Freshman of the Year.

PHENOMS

STAR POWER

898

Points scored by San Diego State's Tina Hutchinson in 1983–84, the mark Watkins broke in 2023–24.

Who is the only unanimous winner of the NFL Defensive Rookie of the Year Award?

After he left Penn State early to enter the 2021 NFL Draft, the Dallas Cowboys were happy to select linebacker **Micah Parsons** with the 12th pick in the first round. But even his new team may have been surprised when Parsons turned in one of the greatest defensive seasons by a rookie in history. In 16 games, he posted a Cowboys rookie record 13.0 sacks along with 84 tackles, and also forced three fumbles. His performance made him the unanimous choice in the Defensive Rookie of the Year balloting. Parsons racked up an additional 39.5 sacks over the next three seasons and has earned four Pro Bowl selections entering the 2025 season.

★ **DID YOU KNOW?** ★

A basketball player in high school, Parsons participated in the NBA All-Star Weekend Celebrity Game in 2024. He scored 37 points and snatched 16 rebounds to lead his team to victory. He was named the game's MVP.

Who won the gold medal in women's park skateboarding at the 2024 Summer Olympics?

Australia has become well known for producing action sports athletes, but few have accomplished more at a younger age than **Arisa Trew**. Trew began skateboarding when she was seven years old, and at 13 became the first female skateboarder to successfully execute a 720 in competition. She won gold in both the women's vert and park competitions at the X Games in 2023, then repeated in 2024. In May of that year, she also became the first female skateboarder to land a 900. That was all prelude to that summer's Olympics in Paris, where Trew won gold in the park event, making her the youngest Australian to ever win a gold medal.

★ **FAST FACT** ★
Trew's parents told her she could get a pet duck if she won gold at the 2024 Summer Olympics. They were true to their word, and she named the duck "Goldie."

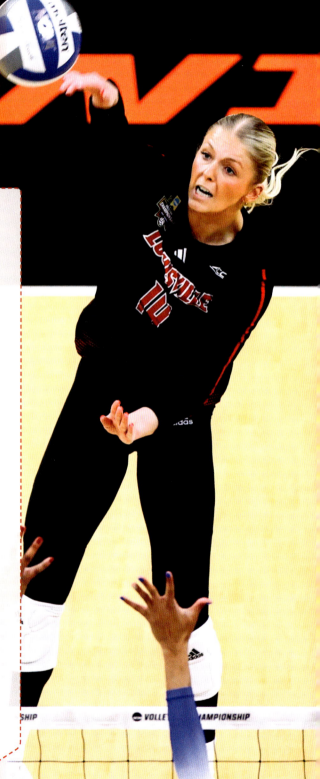

★ **FAST FACT** ★
DeBeer was selected by the Indy Ignite with the second overall pick in the 2024 Pro Volleyball Federation Draft.

Which hometown hero led Louisville to the 2024 NCAA volleyball national championship game?

As a kid growing up in Louisville, Kentucky, **Anna DeBeer** dreamed of one day winning a national championship in volleyball with the Louisville Cardinals. Already a state champion at the high school level, DeBeer continued her winning ways in college and ushered in a golden era for the program. As a sophomore, she helped Louisville reach the Final Four for the first time, then led the team to its first championship game the following year, where they fell to Texas. The outside hitter recorded almost 1,500 kills during her college career, and won three conference championships. Playing for that elusive national championship in 2024, DeBeer was unfortunately injured in the national semifinals and didn't play in the title game, which Louisville lost to Penn State. The loss does nothing to affect her standing as one of the most beloved players in program history.

PHENOMS

★ DID YOU KNOW? ★
Crochet majored in nuclear engineering while a student at the University of Tennessee.

Who tied an AL record by striking out seven batters to start a game in 2024?

Not much went right for the Chicago White Sox in 2024; they set a major league record by losing 121 games, "topping" the record of the 1962 New York Mets, who went 40–120. Perhaps the lone bright spot was left-handed starting pitcher Garrett Crochet. The 11th pick of the 2020 draft, held in June, the 6-foot-6 Crochet was called up that September by the White Sox, the first player in six years to reach the big leagues in the same year he was drafted. After pitching out of the bullpen and battling injuries for several seasons, he moved into the starting rotation in 2024 and finished the season with a 3.58 ERA and 209 strikeouts in 146 innings. An AL All-Star, Crochet struck out seven batters to start a game against the Mets that September, tying a record held by former Chicago pitchers Carlos Rodón (2016) and Joe Cowley (1986), and the Tampa Bay Rays' Blake Snell (2018). In fitting fashion, the White Sox lost that day to the Mets, 2–0. Crochet was traded to Boston that off-season.

RECORD BREAKERS

Who was the first Avalanche defenseman to win the NHL's Norris Trophy?

Colorado Avalanche defenseman **Cale Makar** scored his first NHL goal on his first shot in his first game, against the Calgary Flames during the 2019 Stanley Cup playoffs. Things have only gotten better since, as Makar has blossomed into one of the best players in the league. In his first full season, in 2019–20, he was leading all rookies in scoring before missing time with an injury. He still won the Calder Trophy as the league's best rookie. The following season he finished second in the voting for the Norris Trophy, awarded to the NHL's best defenseman, and then won the Norris after the 2021–22 season. That capped an incredible season for Makar, as he led the Avalanche to victory in the Stanley Cup Final, against the Tampa Bay Lightning, and won the Conn Smythe Trophy as the MVP of the playoffs. He became just the third defenseman to win the Norris and Conn Smythe trophies in the same season, joining Bobby Orr and Nicklas Lidström.

STAR POWER
195
Number of games it took Makar to score 200 career points, the fastest pace of any defenseman in NHL history.

★ FAST FACT ★
Makar was featured on the cover of *NHL 24*, that year's version of the hockey video game series from EA Sports.

RECORD BREAKERS

★ FAST FACT ★
Reese had such a knack for collecting double-doubles, she even posted one in the 2024 WNBA All-Star Game, the first rookie to ever do so.

Who set a WNBA record for most consecutive double-doubles?

Among some casual basketball fans, **Angel Reese** was perhaps best known for her perceived rivalry with fellow WNBA rookie Caitlin Clark. But Reese, the seventh pick of the 2024 WNBA Draft by the Chicago Sky, immediately drew attention with her play on the court, particularly on the defensive end. Reese averaged 13.1 rebounds per game and totaled 446 rebounds, both of which set WNBA single-season records. In a June 4 game against the New York Liberty, the 22-year-old rookie scored 13 points and grabbed 10 boards. It was the start of 15 consecutive games in which Reese notched a double-double; the previous record holder, Candace Parker, posted 12 straight double-doubles at age 24. Though her season was cut short by injury, over 34 games, Reese averaged 13.6 points, 13.1 rebounds, and 1.3 steals.

57

★ **FAST FACT** ★

Thomas graduated from Harvard University with a degree in neurobiology. She also received a master's degree in public health from the University of Texas at Austin.

Who was the only American track athlete to win three gold medals at the 2024 Olympics?

American sprinter Gabby Thomas says that as a child, she was inspired to run after seeing Allyson Felix compete on television. In 2024, at the Olympic Games in Paris, Thomas became the first American woman to win gold in the 200 meters since Felix herself, who won the event at the London Games in 2012. That was just one of three gold medals Thomas won in Paris; she was also part of the winning teams in the 4 x 100 and 4 x 400 meter relay races. It was the culmination of a quest for gold that began in 2020, when Thomas won bronze in the 200 meters and silver in the 4 x 100 relay at the Olympic Games in Tokyo.

58

RECORD BREAKERS

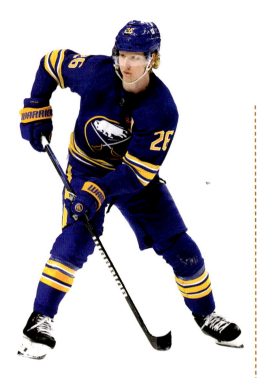

Who was the first defenseman to start an NHL season with a five-game goal streak?

Not since 1989, when the Quebec Nordiques selected Mats Sundin, had a Swedish player been picked first in the NHL draft. **Rasmus Dahlin** became the second Swede to go No. 1 overall, in 2018, and the defenseman has become a cornerstone of the Buffalo Sabres in the years since. A finalist for the Calder Trophy after his rookie season, Dahlin has since been named to three All-Star Games. He started the 2022–23 on fire, when the two-way defenseman made history by scoring goals in the team's first five games of the season.

Who scored the fastest hat trick in USMNT history?

Though he was born in the United States, **Weston McKennie** began playing soccer as a kid in Germany, where his father was stationed as a member of the Air Force. After playing several seasons in that country's Bundesliga, McKennie joined the famed Italian club Juventus—the team's first American player ever. He has played for the U.S. U-17, U-19, and U-20 teams, and was called up to the senior national team in 2017. In a CONCACAF Nations League match against Cuba in 2019, McKennie registered the fastest hat trick from kickoff in USMNT history, scoring three goals in 13 minutes.

59

Who was the first NFL player to score 40 total touchdowns in five consecutive seasons?

The Buffalo Bills thought they had found their next franchise quarterback after picking Wyoming's **Josh Allen** with the seventh pick of the 2018 NFL Draft. He has proven the team right, becoming one of the league's elite QBs. In 2019, Allen led the team to its best record since 1999, and he's only gotten better in the years since. Part of Allen's success is due to his abilities as both a passer and a runner; he has already set a slew of dual-threat records, including most games with 300 yards passing and 50 yards rushing, most games with two passing touchdowns and two rushing touchdowns, as well as becoming the first QB to score touchdowns as a passer, a rusher, and a receiver in a single game. He is also the first player to record 40 or more touchdowns in five straight seasons. In 2025, he was named the NFL MVP.

STAR POWER
135
Allen's total rushing yards in a game against Jacksonville in 2018, the most ever by a Bills quarterback.

★ DID YOU KNOW? ★
Allen is engaged to actress and singer Hailee Steinfeld. They reportedly met in 2023 and went Instagram official that July.

RECORD BREAKERS

> ★ **DID YOU KNOW?** ★
> When it came time to choose a college, Frech decided on USC, becoming the first above-the-knee amputee to commit to a Division I track and field program. "For the little kid who's an amputee who loves track and field to go see someone who looks like him competing at a collegiate level—that's the type of stuff that really excites me," he said.

Who set a Paralympic Games record in the high jump in 2024?

Born with congenital limb differences, **Ezra Frech** had his left leg amputated when he was two years old. That didn't stop him from participating in a variety of sports as a kid, including basketball, soccer, baseball, karate, and, finally, track and field. After watching the 2016 Paralympic Games, Frech vowed to make the U.S. team in 2020, and at the age of 15, he finished fifth in the high jump and eighth in the long jump. He returned at the 2024 Games and finished fifth in the long jump, won gold in the 100m, and then won gold and set a new Paralympic record for T63 athletes—those with the absence of one leg above the knee and who run with a prosthesis—in the high jump.

Who set a WNBA single-season record for three-pointers in 2023?

In 2020, the New York Liberty made **Sabrina Ionescu** the first pick of the WNBA draft. Their belief in the point guard has been well rewarded, as Ionescu helped lead the team to its first championship in 2024. She was a standout performer in college for Oregon, where she was the consensus National Player of the Year and led Division I in assists as a senior. A well-rounded player, she left school as the NCAA career leader in triple-doubles.

Ionescu has displayed an uncanny shooting touch in the WNBA, setting a single-season record for three-pointers in 2023, with 128. She also made headlines in 2024 after competing against Stephen Curry in a three-point contest during the NBA All-Star Weekend. Curry was victorious, scoring 29 points against Ionescu's 26.

RECORD BREAKERS

Who set an MLB record for most hits in a four-game span?

When 19-year-old Seattle Mariners outfielder Julio Rodríguez was looking for someone to play catch with during spring training in 2020, he turned to retired Mariners legend Ichiro Suzuki. The team is certainly hoping that Rodríguez will follow a similar career path after signing him to a massive contract extension that could keep him in Seattle until 2039. As a rookie, Rodríguez was selected to the 2022 All-Star Game and also participated in the Home Run Derby, where he finished second. He ended that season batting .284 with 28 home runs and 25 steals, winning the Silver Slugger and the AL Rookie of the Year awards. In 2023, Rodríguez won his second consecutive Silver Slugger Award and was a finalist for the AL Gold Glove Award in center field. Over four games in August of that year, Rodríguez went 17-for-22, with two home runs and eight RBIs; those 17 hits set an MLB record.

STAR POWER

41

Number of homers hit by Rodríguez in the first round of the 2023 Home Run Derby, setting a record for a single round.

STAR POWER

42

Number of touchdown passes Williams threw for USC in 2022, the most in college football.

Who set Chicago Bears rookie records for touchdowns, yards, and completions in 2024?

No NFL team has been looking for a great quarterback longer than the Chicago Bears. (Arguably the best QB in team history, Sid Luckman, played his last game in 1950.) So it's no surprise fans in the Windy City are excited about **Caleb Williams**. The first overall pick of the 2024 NFL Draft, the former Heisman Trophy winner started all 17 games for the Bears in his rookie season, setting a number of team records in the process. Williams is now the team's single-season rookie leader in touchdowns, yards, completions, passing attempts, passer rating, and rushing yards by a quarterback. He was also the first Bears rookie to pass for more than 300 yards in a game multiple times, highlighted by his 363-yard day against Indianapolis in Week 3. Despite turmoil on the Bears coaching staff and a final record of 5–12, Williams set an NFL rookie record for the most consecutive passing attempts without an interception (354).

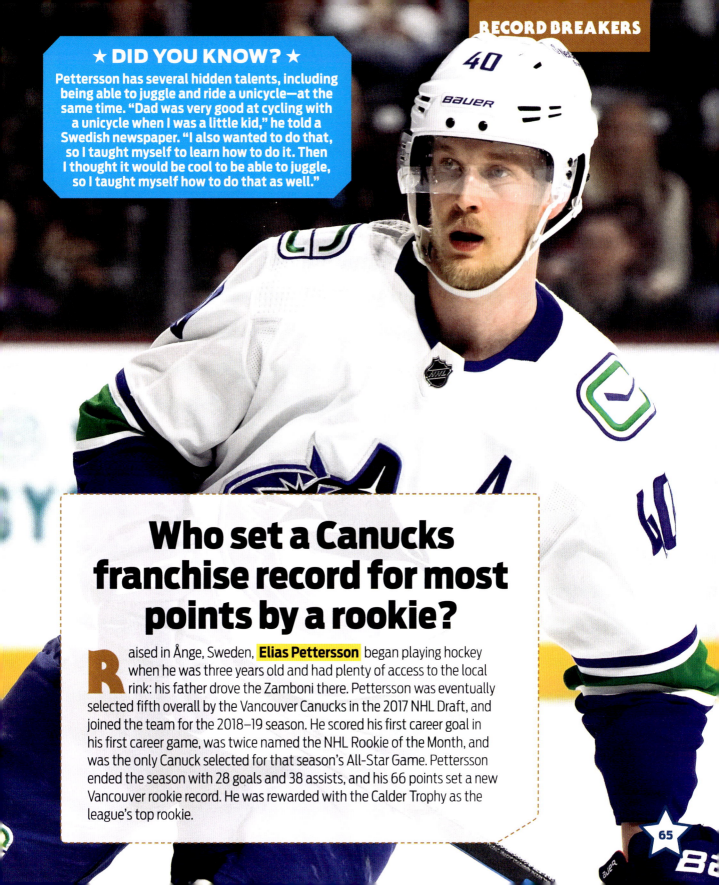

RECORD BREAKERS

★ DID YOU KNOW? ★
Pettersson has several hidden talents, including being able to juggle and ride a unicycle—at the same time. "Dad was very good at cycling with a unicycle when I was a little kid," he told a Swedish newspaper. "I also wanted to do that, so I taught myself to learn how to do it. Then I thought it would be cool to be able to juggle, so I taught myself how to do that as well."

Who set a Canucks franchise record for most points by a rookie?

Raised in Ånge, Sweden, **Elias Pettersson** began playing hockey when he was three years old and had plenty of access to the local rink: his father drove the Zamboni there. Pettersson was eventually selected fifth overall by the Vancouver Canucks in the 2017 NHL Draft, and joined the team for the 2018–19 season. He scored his first career goal in his first career game, was twice named the NHL Rookie of the Month, and was the only Canuck selected for that season's All-Star Game. Pettersson ended the season with 28 goals and 38 assists, and his 66 points set a new Vancouver rookie record. He was rewarded with the Calder Trophy as the league's top rookie.

★ **DID YOU KNOW?** ★
Clark wears No. 22 because she was born on January 22nd. "Honestly, I'm not a very creative person," she joked during a press conference.

RECORD BREAKERS

STAR POWER
55,646
Number of fans at one of Clark's final preseason games at Iowa, a women's basketball attendance record.

★ FAST FACT ★
Clark left Iowa with the highest career scoring average (28.42), the most career points (3,951), and the most three-pointers (548) in Division I history. She also had the second-most triple-doubles (17) and the third-most assists (1,144).

Who is the all-time leading scorer in NCAA Division I basketball history?

In her final regular-season game at the University of Iowa, Caitlin Clark scored 35 points and passed LSU's Pete Maravich as college basketball's all-time leading scorer. But setting records was nothing new for Clark, nor does it capture her impact on the sporting world. A two-time national player of the year, Clark's ability to shoot from anywhere on the floor helped change the sport and made her a must-see attraction. She has become a cultural phenomenon, raising the profile of women's basketball and breaking attendance and viewership records everywhere she played; Clark's final three games of the 2024 NCAA tournament each broke the women's college basketball viewership record, including the 18.9 million viewers who tuned in for the national championship game. It was the first time the women's tournament final outdrew the men's. Clark was selected No. 1 overall in the 2024 WNBA draft by the Indiana Fever. In her first professional season, she led the league in assists, was named to the All-WNBA First Team, and was Rookie of the Year.

Who was the first American gymnast to win a gold medal in pommel horse at the World Championships?

Though he began his gymnastics career competing on all apparatuses, **Stephen Nedoroscik** decided to specialize on pommel horse when he was in high school. It proved to be a wise choice, as Nedoroscik was the NCAA national champion in that event in 2017 and 2018, and finished second in 2019. At the 2021 World Championships, Nedoroscik won the world title on pommel horse, the first American to ever do so. His fame truly skyrocketed at the 2024 Olympic Games in Paris, where his final routine clinched a bronze medal for the U.S. in the team final; he also won the bronze in the individual competition. Fans on social media dubbed him "Pommel Horse Guy" and compared the removal of his glasses just before performing to Clark Kent taking off his glasses before transforming into Superman.

★ DID YOU KNOW? ★

Nedoroscik has an eye condition that leaves his pupils permanently dilated and necessitates the wearing of glasses. It didn't stop him from winning two Olympic medals, or from graduating from Penn State University with a degree in electrical engineering.

STAR POWER

61

Nix's number of combined starts in college for Auburn and Oregon, more than any quarterback in NCAA history.

Who set a Denver Broncos single-season rookie record for most touchdown passes?

The Denver Broncos are no strangers to having a great quarterback; after all, their history includes both John Elway and Peyton Manning. So when the team selected **Bo Nix** with the 12th pick of the 2024 NFL Draft, expectations were high. Nix had led the nation in completions and touchdown passes with the Oregon Ducks in 2023, and his accuracy made him attractive to Denver's coach Sean Payton. He started all 17 games for the team in 2024, finishing the season with 29 touchdown passes, a franchise record for rookies. (It was also the second-most by any NFL rookie, behind only Justin Herbert's 31 in 2020.) Despite being the sixth QB chosen in his draft class, Nix led all rookies in completions, passing yards, touchdown passes, and total touchdowns, as the Broncos returned to the playoffs for the first time since 2015.

Which quarterback set the NFL rookie record for most completions in a season?

When Los Angeles Chargers quarterback **Justin Herbert** showed up for work on the second Sunday of his rookie season in 2020, he was ready to wait his turn behind starting QB Tyrod Taylor. But when Taylor was unable to take the field against the Kansas City Chiefs, the sixth-overall draft pick was ready. Herbert threw for 311 yards in his NFL debut, and by the end of the season, he had completed 396 passes, the most ever by a rookie quarterback. He also set the rookie record for most touchdown passes, with 31. In the years since, Herbert has developed into one of the game's best QBs, completing a career-best 477 passes in 2022.

RECORD BREAKERS

★ FAST FACT ★
Lyles is a fan of manga and anime. His favorites include *Full Metal Alchemist* and *Cage of Eden*.

Who won the fastest overall 100 meter race in Olympic history?

Heading into the 2024 Summer Olympics in Paris, the last American man to win Olympic gold in the 100 meters was Justin Gatlin, in 2004. Noah Lyles planned to change that, and he wasn't shy about letting everyone know it. Already a three-time winner in the 200 meters at the World Championships, Lyles decided to also run in the 100 meters at the Olympics, and attempt to win gold in both events, a feat not accomplished by an American since Carl Lewis, in 1984. His quest got off to a fast start, as he won the 100 meters in historic fashion; his personal best time of 9.784 was 0.005 seconds faster than Jamaica's Kishane Thompson, making for perhaps the closest finish in the event's history. It was also the first time in history that the entire field broke the 10-second barrier. Two days before he ran in the 200 meters, Lyles tested positive for COVID-19, which seemingly affected his performance; nonetheless, he finished in third to take home the bronze.

STAR POWER
0.12 SECONDS
The gap between first place and last place in the 100 meters at the 2024 Summer Olympics, the closest race in history.

71

STAR POWER

4.21 MILLION

Number of views Morant's game-winner against the Spurs amassed on the NBA's Instagram account, the most ever to that point.

RECORD BREAKERS

Who was the first Memphis Grizzlies player to score 50 points in a game?

Entering the 2019 NBA Draft, most fans had their eyes on the eventual No. 1 overall pick, Duke's Zion Williamson. The second selection belonged to the Memphis Grizzlies, who wisely selected **Ja Morant** from Murray State. The lightning-quick point guard recorded his first career triple-double the following February, was selected for the Rising Stars Game at the All-Star break, and was named the league's Rookie of the Year after leading his class in assists and points scored. The following year, he led the Grizzlies to their first postseason appearance in four seasons. Morant truly broke out in 2021–22, leading Memphis to its first Southwest Division title and tying the franchise record with 56 wins. In a February game against San Antonio, Morant scored 52 points, becoming the first Memphis player to score more than 50 in a game.

★ FAST FACT ★

Morant has worn the number 12 in high school, college, and the NBA. His jersey was retired at both Crestwood High School in South Carolina and at Murray State in Kentucky.

STAR POWER

8

Number of quarterbacks selected before Purdy in the 2022 NFL Draft.

Who holds the 49ers' record for most passing yards in a season?

Each year, the player selected with the very last pick in the NFL Draft is referred to as "Mr. Irrelevant," because few expect him to contribute much to his new team. **Brock Purdy** was determined to change that perception. After being chosen by San Francisco with the 262nd pick in 2022, Purdy won all five of his starts and became the lowest-drafted QB ever to win a playoff game. Entering the 2023 season, Purdy was the unquestioned starter and threw for 4,280 yards, besting the previous franchise record set by Jeff Garcia. Purdy then became the lowest-drafted quarterback to start a Super Bowl, during which the 49ers fell to the Kansas City Chiefs 25–22 in SB LVIII.

RECORD BREAKERS

Who was the first Italian player to reach the top of the ATP rankings?

Few tennis players have followed as unique a path to stardom as **Jannik Sinner**. Born in a small village in northern Italy, Sinner grew up speaking German and skiing competitively; in fact, he won a national championship in giant slalom at the age of eight. But he was also interested in tennis, and by the time he was 16 he had started competing in professional tournaments. By the time he turned 17, he had already won several ATP Challenger Tour titles. In 2020, he became the youngest quarterfinalist at the French Open since Novak Djokovic in 2006, then truly broke out in 2023–24, reaching the semis at Wimbledon in '23 and the French Open in '24, and winning the Australian and U.S. opens in '24. Sinner climbed to the top of the world rankings for the first time that June, the first Italian player to hold the top position, surpassing Adriano Panatta's career-high of No. 4 in 1976.

★ DID YOU KNOW? ★
Sinner's distinctive red hair has earned him the nickname "The Fox." His fans, known as the Carota Boys, often cheer him on dressed in carrot costumes. (Carota means carrot in French.)

75

RECORD BREAKERS

Which quarterback set an NFL rookie record for most rushing yards in a season?

The Washington Commanders entered the 2024 season looking for a change in fortune. The team, which had been sold to new ownership in 2023, was coming off seven straight seasons without a winning record, and had only won 10 games in a season twice this century. Enter **Jayden Daniels**, the 2023 Heisman Trophy winner and second overall pick in the 2024 NFL Draft. Daniels earned the starting QB job during training camp, then set a rookie completion percentage record (91.3%) against the Cincinnati Bengals that September, and was named Offensive Rookie of the Month. Five weeks later, he cemented his must-see status by throwing a game-winning 52-yard Hail Mary pass against the Chicago Bears. Daniels finished the regular season with the most rushing yards (891) and highest completion percentage (69%) ever posted by a rookie quarterback, as the Commanders went 12–5, their best record since 1991. Daniels then led the team to postseason victories over Tampa Bay and Detroit before falling in the NFC Championship Game against Philadelphia.

★ **DID YOU KNOW?** ★

Daniels was featured on *The Money Game: LSU*, a docuseries that followed him, Alia Armstrong, Livvy Dunne, Flau'jae Johnson, Angel Reese, and Trace Young during LSU's 2023–24 sports season.

STAR POWER

12

Number of fourth-quarter and overtime touchdown passes by Daniels in 2024, an NFL rookie record.

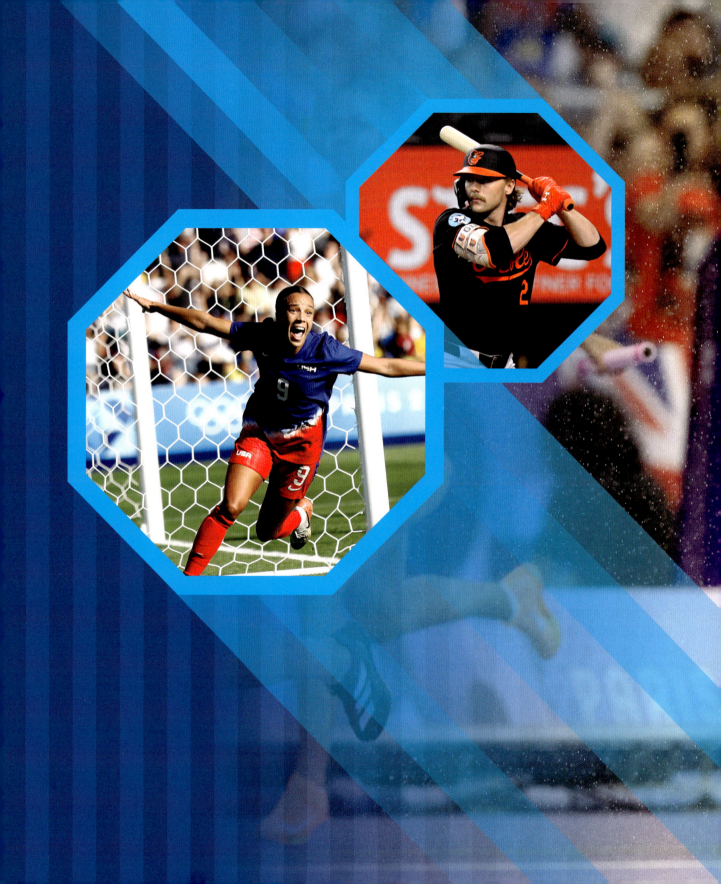

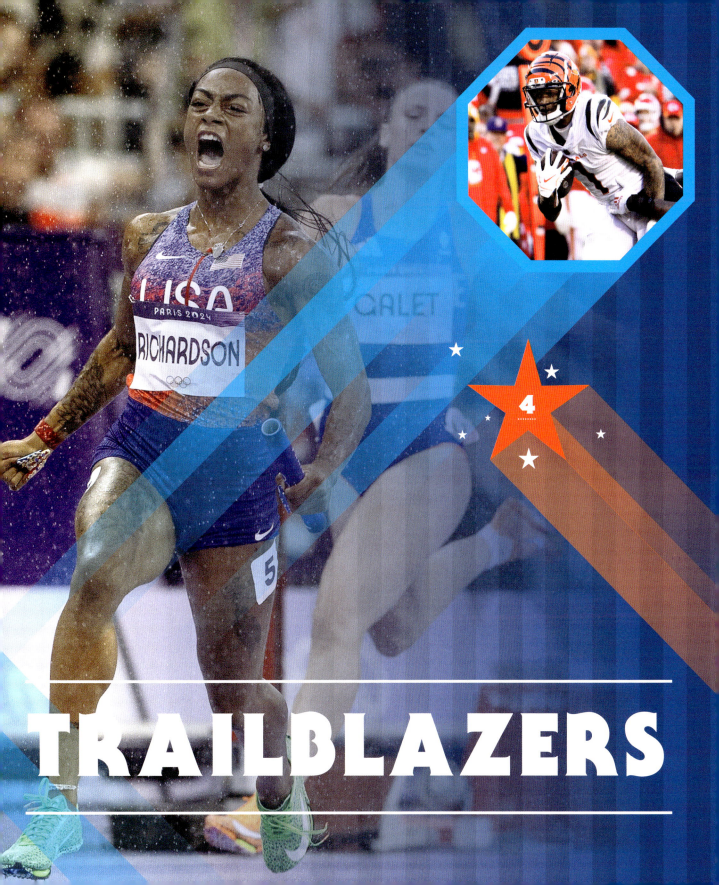

TRAILBLAZERS

4

Who was the first European-born player to lead the NBA in scoring?

By the time he reached the NBA in 2018, **Luka Dončić** was one of the most accomplished European players in history. The son of a former Slovenia player and coach, Dončić made his professional debut for Real Madrid in the Liga ACB at the age of 16, and when his career in Spain was over, he was a three-time champion and the youngest player to win an ACB title, a EuroLeague title, the EuroLeague MVP, and the EuroLeague Final Four MVP. He was selected third overall and traded to the Dallas Mavericks in the 2018 NBA Draft and was named the Rookie of the Year at the end of the season. Dončić has only gotten better in the years since, and was named to five consecutive All-Star Games and five All-NBA First Teams entering the 2024–25 season. In 2023–24, he led the Mavericks to the NBA Finals after leading the league in scoring with a 33.9 points-per-game average. He became the first player born in Europe to achieve that feat, and just the second international player to do so. (Cameroon-born Joel Embiid of the Philadelphia 76ers is the other.) Dončić was shockingly traded to the Los Angeles Lakers in 2025.

★ **DID YOU KNOW?** ★
Dončić is a gamer who has enjoyed playing *Call of Duty*, *FIFA*, and *Overwatch*. He was a top 500 player in *Overwatch 2*.

★ **FAST FACT** ★
Dončić speaks four different languages: English, Slovenian, Spanish, and Serbian.

TRAIL BLAZERS

STAR POWER

66

Points Heise scored during her senior collegiate season at Minnesota, in 2021–22. She tallied 29 goals and 37 assists in just 39 games.

Who was the inaugural PWHL Playoff MVP?

The first season of the Professional Women's Hockey League was a whirlwind for forward **Taylor Heise**. At the University of Minnesota, Heise led the nation in total points as a senior; she was also part of three gold medal winning teams at the World U18 Championships representing the United States. In the NWHL's inaugural draft in 2023, Heise was the No. 1 pick by the Minnesota franchise. She scored her first career professional goal in Minnesota's first game, and finished the 19-game regular season with four goals and nine assists. She turned things up in the playoffs, leading her team with five goals and three assists over 10 games as Minnesota won the league's first championship. She was named the Ilana Kloss Playoff MVP for her performance.

TRAIL BLAZERS

★ **FAST FACT** ★

Breakker isn't the only WWE performer with professional football experience. Other former football stars include Roman Reigns, Goldberg, and Dwayne "The Rock" Johnson.

Which WWE Superstar is related to the famous Steiner Brothers tag team?

If you thought current WWE Superstar **Bron Breakker** looked familiar, you're not mistaken. Breakker, whose real name is Bronson Rechsteiner, is the son of Rick Steiner and the nephew of Scott Steiner, two wrestling legends who performed for decades, often together as the Steiner Brothers. Today, Breakker is making his own name in the ring. After playing football in college and signing as an undrafted free agent with the NFL's Baltimore Ravens, Breakker went into the family business, signing with the WWE in 2021. In the years since, he's won the NXT Championship, the NXT Tag Team Championship, and the WWE Intercontinental Championship.

★ DID YOU KNOW? ★
Henderson used Motley Crue's "Kickstart My Heart" as his walkup song in the minors, but switched to Gwen Stefani's "The Sweet Escape" when he made it to the big leagues.

Who was the unanimous 2023 AL Rookie of the Year?

Entering the 2019 MLB Draft, Alabama native **Gunnar Henderson** was projected to be a mid-first-round pick. Instead, the Baltimore Orioles made the infielder the first selection of the second round, and soon the other teams would recognize their mistake. Henderson was named the Baseball America Minor League Player of the Year and made his major league debut in 2022, then made Baltimore's Opening Day roster in 2023. He ended up leading the Orioles in Wins Above Replacement and ranked first among AL rookies in home runs (28), triples (nine), RBIs (82), and runs scored (100). He was unanimously voted the AL Rookie of the Year, the first Oriole to win that award in 34 years. In 2024, he took another step toward superstardom, batting .281 with 37 home runs and 92 RBIs. The Orioles made the postseason in both '23 and '24, with the local media naming Henderson the Most Valuable Oriole in both seasons.

TRAIL BLAZERS

★ FAST FACT ★

Four Orioles have hit at least 30 home runs and stolen 20 bases in a season: Henderson (37 and 21 in 2024); Cedric Mullins (30 and 30 in 2021); Manny Machado (35 and 20 in 2015); and Brady Anderson (50 and 21 in 1996).

Who anchored the women's 4 x 100 meter relay team to a gold medal at the 2024 Olympics?

All eyes were on world champion sprinter **Sha'Carri Richardson** at the 2024 Olympic Games in Paris. After all, she had just won gold in the 100 meters and as part of the women's 4 × 100 relay team at the 2023 World Championships, setting championship records in both events. The two-time U.S. national champion in the 100 sprint fell just short of gold at the Olympics, finishing second behind Saint Lucia's Julien Alfred to claim the silver medal. But Richardson had another shot at gold in the 4 x 100 relay, and she wasn't about to let it go to waste. After some trouble passing the baton, Team USA entered the final leg behind Germany and Great Britain, but Richardson took it from there, roaring past her competition to claim gold. Her side-eyed glance at her fellow runners became one of the indelible moments of that year's Games.

★ **DID YOU KNOW?** ★
Lawrence and his wife, Marissa, have known each other since the fifth grade. They were married in 2021.

STAR POWER

332

Passing yards Lawrence collected in his first career start, against the Houston Texans in 2021, an AFC rookie record.

Who is the youngest player to throw four touchdown passes in an NFL postseason game?

Expectations were high when the Jacksonville Jaguars selected quarterback **Trevor Lawrence** with the first pick in the 2021 NFL Draft. That was understandable, considering Lawrence went 34–2 as a starter and won a national championship while at Clemson University. After an underwhelming rookie year, Lawrence notably improved in his second season, leading the Jaguars to seven wins in their last nine games. The highlight of that season came in the wild card round against the Los Angeles Chargers. Lawrence threw four interceptions in the first half as the Chargers jumped out to a seemingly unsurmountable 27–0 lead. But the quarterback rebounded to throw three touchdown passes in the second half and earn a 31–30 victory, the third-largest comeback in NFL playoff history. Combined with the touchdown pass he threw in the first half, Lawrence became the youngest player to throw four touchdowns in a playoff game, at 23 years and 100 days.

TRAIL BLAZERS

Who is the most recent Detroit Tigers pitcher to win the Triple Crown?

The Detroit Tigers have been home to many excellent starting pitchers throughout their history, from Denny McLain to Justin Verlander. The latest to claim the mantle as staff ace is **Tarik Skubal**. A ninth-round pick in the 2018 MLB Draft, Skubal impressed the Tigers enough for them to put him in their starting rotation in 2021, but his next two seasons were derailed by injuries. Back at full strength in 2024, he had a historic season; an All-Star selection during the summer, Skubal led the league with 18 wins, a 2.39 ERA, and 228 strikeouts, becoming the first pitcher to win the Triple Crown in a full season since Verlander (AL) and the Dodgers' Clayton Kershaw (NL) did in 2011.

TRAIL BLAZERS

STAR POWER

5,899

Jefferson's receiving yards total through his first four seasons, the most in NFL history.

Who is the youngest player to lead the NFL in receiving yards?

When the Minnesota Vikings selected Justin Jefferson with the 22nd pick of the 2020 NFL Draft, they hoped he would someday join past wide receivers Cris Carter and Randy Moss among the franchise's greats. They may have been surprised when he immediately began rewriting the record books, setting the NFL mark for most receiving yards (1,400) by a rookie on his way to being named to the Pro Bowl. He followed that up with 1,616 receiving yards to set the record for most receiving yards in a player's first two seasons. In 2022, he led the league with 128 receptions for 1,809 yards, becoming the youngest ever to lead the NFL in those categories, at the age of 23. Despite missing seven games due to injury during the 2023 season, Jefferson still racked up 1,074 yards receiving.

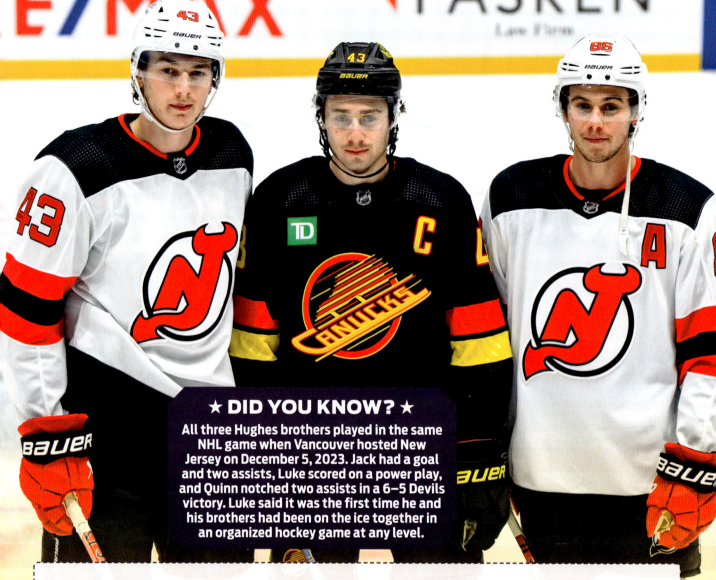

★ DID YOU KNOW? ★
All three Hughes brothers played in the same NHL game when Vancouver hosted New Jersey on December 5, 2023. Jack had a goal and two assists, Luke scored on a power play, and Quinn notched two assists in a 6–5 Devils victory. Luke said it was the first time he and his brothers had been on the ice together in an organized hockey game at any level.

Which American family has had three players selected in the first round of the NHL draft?

Hockey history is littered with famous siblings, from Maurice and Henri Richard to the Sutter brothers to the Sedin twins. You can add **Quinn**, **Jack**, and **Luke Hughes** to that illustrious list. Quinn, the oldest, was the seventh pick in 2018 by Vancouver; he was a finalist for the Calder Trophy and won the Norris Trophy as the league's best defenseman in 2024. Jack was the first overall selection in 2019, and is a three-time All-Star for the Calgary Flames. Quinn and Jack's younger brother Luke was the Devils' fourth-overall selection in 2021, and in 2023–24 led rookie defensemen in power-play points, and was named a finalist for the Calder Trophy and was voted unanimously to the All-Rookie Team.

TRAIL BLAZERS

STAR POWER

38

National team goals scored by Swanson through the 2024 Summer Olympics.

Who scored the gold medal winning goal for the USWNT at the 2024 Olympics?

Soccer forward **Mallory Swanson** began playing the game because she wanted to be like her older sister, Brianna. The U.S. Women's National Team is glad she did, because Swanson has become an integral part of the program's success in international tournaments. After playing for the U.S. at the under-17 and under-20 levels, in 2016 Swanson became the youngest American to score a goal at the Olympics, in Rio de Janeiro, at the age of 18. The U.S. failed to medal in those Games, and Swanson was dealing with injuries during the team's run to a bronze in 2020, meaning the 2024 Paris Games gave her another shot at gold. Swanson did not miss her chance, scoring the game-winning goal in the 57th minute against Brazil to clinch the tournament for the Americans.

★ **FAST FACT** ★

Swanson is married to Major League Baseball shortstop Dansby Swanson.

★ FAST FACT ★
Morikawa is a two-time Olympian, competing for the United States at the 2020 Games in Tokyo and the 2024 Games in Paris.

Who started his PGA Tour career with 22 consecutive made cuts?

A native of Los Angeles, Collin Morikawa began playing golf at the age of five. By the time he was done playing collegiately at the University of California–Berkeley, he had won five events, including the 2019 Pac-12 Conference Championship, and had finished his junior season as the nation's top-ranked golfer. He wasted little time once he turned pro in 2019, safely making the cut in 22 straight tournaments, second in PGA history only to Tiger Woods, who began his career with 25. In 2020, he won the PGA Championship in his first appearance at that event, then did likewise at the 2021 Open Championship in England, becoming the only golfer to win two different majors in his debut appearance. He has been listed as high as No. 2 in the Official Golf World Ranking.

TRAIL BLAZERS

Who was the first USMNT player to appear in a game for Barcelona?

The Barcelona football club is one of the most prestigious teams in the world. Winners of more than 20 European and worldwide titles, including five UEFA Champions League championships, they enjoy one of the largest fan followings in the world. Playing for Barcelona is an honor among soccer players, which makes the appearance of **Sergiño Dest** in 2020 so notable; he became the first American to ever play for the club since its founding in 1899. Dest has also played in Italy and the Netherlands, and has been a critical part of the USMNT in international play since 2019.

Who was the first Packers quarterback to lead them to the playoffs in his first season as the starter?

Quarterback **Jordan Love** had huge shoes to fill when he took over as the starting quarterback of the Green Bay Packers in 2023. After all, he was replacing future Hall of Famer Aaron Rodgers, who himself had replaced Hall of Famer Brett Favre. In Love's first start of the season, he threw for 245 yards and three touchdowns, but the team was just 8–8 heading into its season finale, a game Green Bay needed to win to guarantee its playoff spot. Love came through, leading the Packers to a 17–9 victory over the Chicago Bears. He finished the season with 4,159 passing yards and 32 touchdown passes. In his first playoff game, against the Dallas Cowboys, Love posted a near-perfect passer rating of 157.2 as the Packers became the first No. 7 seed to win a postseason game. In July 2024, he signed one of the largest contracts in NFL history.

STAR POWER

$500,000

The amount Dunne said she was paid for a single social media post, in July 2023.

TRAIL BLAZERS

Which NCAA gymnastics champion has more than 13 million social media followers?

In 2021, the NCAA changed its rules to allow college athletes to earn money from their name, image, and likeness (NIL). Few athletes have taken better advantage of this new world than **Livvy Dunne**, a Scholastic All-American gymnast from Louisiana State University. Originally from New Jersey, Dunne joined the LSU gymnastics team in 2020, and despite battling injuries throughout her career she competed in nine meets for the Tigers in 2024 as the team won a national championship. Dunne has been even more impressive outside the gym, where her followers on TikTok (8 million) and Instagram (5 million) make her one of the nation's most marketable athletes.

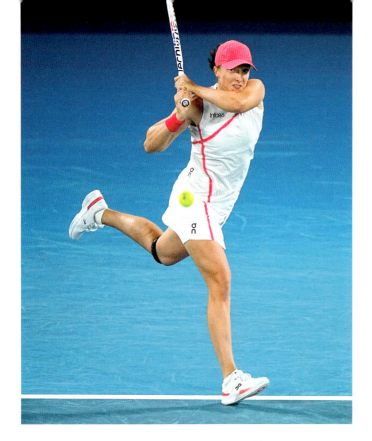

Who was the first Polish player to win a major tournament on the WTA Tour?

Despite not joining the WTA Tour until 2019, it's quite possible that **Iga Świątek** is already the greatest Polish tennis player in history. Born in Warsaw, Świątek and her sister began playing tennis at a young age, and by 17 Iga had won the Junior championship at WImbledon. In 2020, Świątek was ranked No. 54 in the world entering that year's French Open, but defeated sixth-ranked Sofia Kenin in the final to become the first Polish player to win a major singles title and the lowest-ranked French Open champion in WTA history. Świątek has made the tournament at Roland Garros her own in the years since, winning three more French Open titles, as well as a championship at the U.S. Open, in 2022. She finished as the top-ranked woman in the world in both 2022 and 2023.

Who was the youngest captain at the 2022 FIFA World Cup?

Entering the 2022 FIFA World Cup, the USMNT boasted headliner names including Christian Pulisic and Weston McKennie. But when it came time for the players to vote on a captain, it was **Tyler Adams** who was selected to wear the armband, making him the youngest captain in the tournament and the youngest American captain since 1950. A homegrown player of the MLS's New York Red Bulls, Adams has also played in Germany's Bundesliga and the English Premier League. His teammate, McKennie, knew Adams was a natural-born leader. "What's amazing about it is that even whenever he doesn't wear the captain's armband, sometimes you still get a sense of his leadership role that he takes on within the team," McKennie said.

TRAIL BLAZERS

STAR POWER

50.37

McLaughlin-Levrone's world record time in the 400 meter hurdles at the 2024 Summer Olympics, breaking her own world record of 50.65.

Who was the first track athlete to break four world records in the same event?

Few runners have ever dominated a track and field event like **Sydney McLaughlin-Levrone**. A specialist in the 400 meter hurdles, McLaughlin-Levrone has been hard to beat since she set a national high school freshman record in the event back in 2014. She has won the gold medal or finished first six times in competitions since 2015, including at the World Youth Championships (2015), the Diamond League (2019), and the World Championships (2019, 2022). After winning gold at the 2020 Olympics, she became the first woman ever to repeat as champion of the event at the 2024 Games in Paris. Her winning time in France was a new world record, the fourth time McLaughlin-Levrone had managed that feat. She also won gold medals as part of the U.S. 400 meter relay team in both 2020 and 2024.

★ FAST FACT ★
Malinin's Instagram handle is "ilia_quadg0d_malinin," a reference to his "Quad God" nickname.

Who is the first figure skater to land a quad Axel?

American-born figure skater **Ilia Malinin** is doing things no one in his sport has ever done. The son of two Olympic Uzbekistani skaters, Malinin was on the ice by the age of six and won the 2022 World Junior Championships while setting records for the short program, the free skate, and total score. He won again at the 2023 U.S. Figure Skating Championships, and repeated the feat in 2024 and 2025. Malinin also won gold at the 2024 World Championships and is favored to win gold again at the Winter Olympics in 2026. One reason for all this success is his mastery of quad jumps, in which the skater jumps and rotates four times in the air. Malinin is the only skater to land a quad Axel, in which he rotated four and a half times.

TRAIL BLAZERS

STAR POWER
16
Age at which Matson was selected for the U.S. Women's National Team, only the second player to be chosen at that age. (First was Katie Bam, in 2005.)

Which field hockey star won four NCAA titles as a player and another as a head coach?

It's possible that **Erin Matson** is already the most accomplished field hockey star of all time. Referred to as "the Michael Jordan of field hockey" by her college coach, Matson won four national championships at the University of North Carolina as a player, and graduated as the Atlantic Coast Conference's all-time leading scorer in goals and points. She was named the nation's best player three times, and led the Tar Heels to a 99–8 record that included three undefeated seasons. When her collegiate playing career was finished, UNC hired her to be its new head coach, despite Matson being just 22 years old. In her first season, coaching players who a year prior had been her teammates, Matson led the team to yet another national championship.

101

STAR POWER
1,823
Chase's receiving yards during the 2021 season, including the postseason, the most ever by a rookie.

Who set an NFL rookie record for most receiving yards in a game?

As teammates at Louisiana State University in 2019, quarterback Joe Burrow and receiver **Ja'Marr Chase** were electrifying; Chase racked up 84 receptions for 1,780 yards and 20 touchdowns as the Tigers won the national championship. In 2021, the Cincinnati Bengals, who already had Burrow under center, drafted Chase with the fifth pick in that year's draft, reuniting this dynamic duo. They picked up where they left off, as Chase set a slew of rookie receiving records, including being the youngest player to catch four touchdown passes through his first three games and the most receiving yards in a player's first seven games (754). In a late-season matchup against the Kansas City Chiefs, Chase racked up 266 receiving yards and caught three touchdowns in Cincinnati's 34–31 division-clinching win. Those 266 yards were the most ever by a rookie in a single game.

TRAIL BLAZERS

Who is the youngest woman to win an Olympic snowboarding gold medal?

Competing at her first Olympics, the 2018 Pyeongchang Games, **Chloe Kim** became the youngest woman to win an Olympic snowboarding gold medal at 17 years and 296 days. The previous record holder, Kelly Clark, was 18 when she won gold at Salt Lake City 2002. Kim's score of 93.75 on her first run secured her win, as none of the women in the field could top it through two remaining runs. With her gold medal already assured, Kim attempted and landed back-to-back 1080s (three full rotations) on her final run, becoming the first woman to do so at the Olympics.

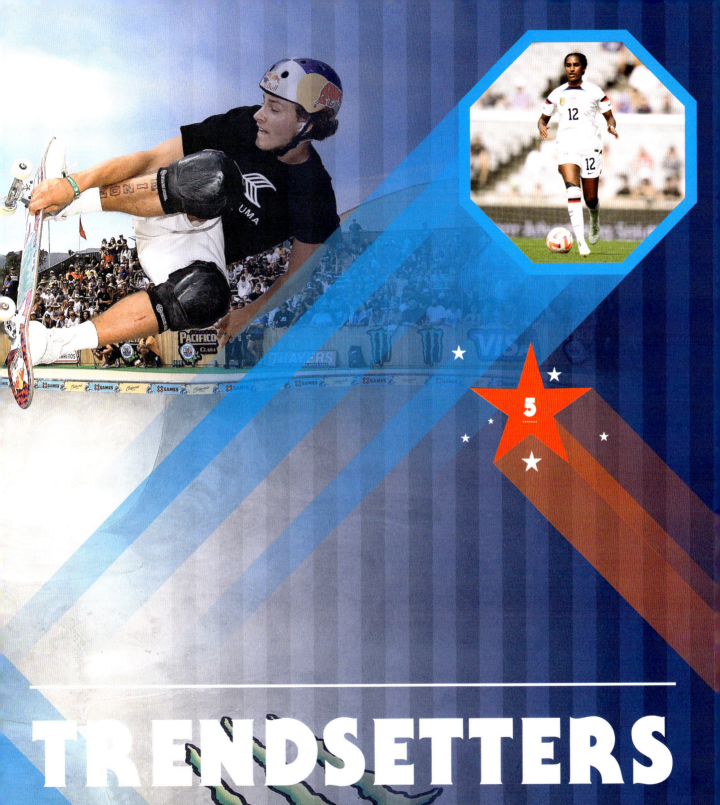

STAR POWER
20.6
Canady's scoring average in her final year playing high school basketball. She was named All-State in all three years she played.

Which college softball player was the first to sign a $1 million NIL deal?

When reigning USA Softball Collegiate Player of the Year **NiJaree Canady** announced in 2024 that she would be transferring from Stanford University, it obviously generated plenty of media coverage. But few people were prepared for the next set of headlines: Canady had signed a one-year, $1 million NIL deal to play for Texas Tech, the highest ever for a college softball player. It's hard to argue Canady wasn't worth it: a two-time Kansas high school player of the year, she had a 41–10 record, a 0.66 ERA, and 555 strikeouts with 65 walks in 366⅔ innings while at Stanford. Still, few expected any NIL collective to make such an investment in a softball player, including Canady herself. "I just feel like I found a school that really invested in women's sports," Canaday said at a Women in Sports seminar, "and found a program and community who wants to invest in women's sports."

TRENDSETTERS

Which NBA All-Star released his own signature shoe while still in high school?

Charlotte Hornets guard **LaMelo Ball** charted a unique course to NBA stardom. By the time he was four years old, LaMelo and his brothers, Lonzo and LiAngelo, were being trained by their father, LaVar. In addition to their on-court skills, LaVar was also focused on maximizing his sons' future professional opportunities, so after LaMelo finished his sophomore high school season averaging 26.7 points and almost 10 assists per game, he decided to play professionally in Europe rather than enroll in college. In addition, Big Baller Brand, his family's sports apparel company, released the Melo Ball 1, making him the first high schooler to have his own shoe. None of this precluded the Hornets from selecting Ball with the third pick of the 2020 NBA Draft. He was the league's Rookie of the Year in 2021 and was named an Eastern Conference All-Star in 2022.

★ FAST FACT ★
Prior to the NBA, Ball played for BC Birštono Vytautas in the Lithuanian Basketball League and the Los Angeles Ballers in the Junior Basketball Association (2018), as well as the Illawarra Hawks in Australia's National Basketball League (2019–20).

★ DID YOU KNOW? ★

Born in Toronto, Canada, Gilgeous-Alexander's full name is Shaivonte Aician Gilgeous-Alexander. His mother, Charmaine Gilgeous, ran track in the 1992 Summer Olympics, and his father, Vaughn Alexander, was his youth basketball coach.

TRENDSETTERS

Who is the youngest NBA guard to average 30 points while shooting 50 percent from the field?

At the outset of his NBA career, **Shai Gilgeous-Alexander** was perhaps best known as part of the trade that sent All-Star Paul George to the Los Angeles Clippers in 2019. But it didn't take long for Gilgeous-Alexander to make his own mark in the league with the Oklahoma City Thunder. Thanks to his silky moves and selfless play, he made the All-Star team in 2023, 2024, and 2025 and was also named First Team All-NBA all three years. During that 2023 season, he joined Michael Jordan as the only guards to average at least 30 points, four rebounds, four assists, one block, and one steal while shooting at least 50 percent from the field. He also became the youngest guard to average 30 points on 50 percent from the field in NBA history. In 2024, Gilgeous-Alexander finished second in the MVP voting behind three-time winner Nikola Jokić.

★ FAST FACT ★
Well known for his fashionable tunnel fits, *GQ* magazine named Gilgeous-Alexander the Most Stylish NBA Player in 2022 and 2023.

Who scored the first hat trick in PWHL history?

The debut season of the Professional Women's Hockey League, held in 2023–24, was filled with firsts. Two of those firsts belong to **Grace Zumwinkle**, a forward for the Minnesota Frost. Zumwinkle played college hockey at the University of Minnesota, leading her team in scoring as a freshman and serving as its co-captain as a senior. She was drafted 13th overall in the PWHL's inaugural draft, and she scored three goals in Minnesota's first ever home game, the first hat trick in league history. At the end of the season, she was named the league's first Rookie of the Year. Zumwinkle has also represented the United States three times at the World Championships and once at the 2022 Olympic Games, earning silver medals in each appearance.

STAR POWER

19

Points scored by Zumwinkle for Minnesota in 2023–24, most on the team.

TRENDSETTERS

★ **FAST FACT** ★
Johnson has signed NIL deals with brands including Puma, JBL, and Taco Bell, making her one of college basketball's top earners.

Which college basketball star also has a record deal with Roc Nation?

When Angel Reese graduated from LSU in 2024, the women's basketball team lost one of the most recognizable faces in the game today. Enter **Flau'jae Johnson**, who was more than ready to step into the spotlight. After playing in the McDonald's All-American Game as a high schooler, Johnson averaged 11 points per game as a freshman and helped lead the Tigers to their first national championship. The following season, she consistently led the team in scoring in the NCAA tournament before falling in the Elite Eight. Johnson is a star off the court as well; the daughter of famed recording artist Camouflage, she signed a distribution deal with Jay-Z's Roc Nation in 2023. Her album *Best of Both Worlds* was released in 2024.

★ **DID YOU KNOW?** ★

Witt Jr.'s father had a 16-year career pitching in the major leagues. Witt Jr. also has three brothers-in-law who played in the majors: Zach Neal, James Russell, and Cody Thomas.

Who was the first MLB shortstop to post two 30-30 seasons?

Traditionally, shortstops have often been smaller, faster players who were good with the glove and stole some bases. In the late 1990s, bigger players such as Alex Rodriguez began to hit home runs at a rate more often seen among first basemen. Few shortstops blend speed and power better than the Kansas City Royals' **Bobby Witt Jr.** Considered one of the top prospects in baseball, Witt Jr. was selected second overall in the 2019 MLB Draft and made his big-league debut in 2022. He finished that season with 20 home runs and 30 steals, making him the fifth player in MLB history to hit at least 20 home runs and steal at least 20 bases in their first season. The following year, he upped his totals to 30 home runs and 49 stolen bases. In 2024, Witt Jr. had an MVP-level season, leading the AL in batting average (.332) and hits (211) while hitting 32 home runs and stealing 31 bases, making him the first shortstop to post two 30-30 seasons. He is also the first player to go 20-20 in his first three seasons.

TRENDSETTERS

Who was the first NCAA athlete to take an ownership share in a professional league?

The introduction of name, image, and likeness deals has changed the face of college sports. One athlete who has taken advantage of this new environment is UConn Huskies guard **Paige Bueckers**. The No. 1 recruit in her high school class, Bueckers left her home state of Minnesota in 2020 to play in Storrs, Connecticut, and became the first freshman to win a major national women's college player of the year award as she led UConn to the Final Four of the NCAA tournament. After missing most of her sophomore and all of her junior season due to injuries, she returned in 2023–24 and again helped her team reach the Final Four, averaging 21.9 points per game. Before beginning her final college season in 2024–25, Bueckers signed a deal with Unrivaled, a three-on-three professional league, that will earn her ownership equity once she joins a team following her first WNBA season.

★ DID YOU KNOW? ★

Bueckers has won four gold medals representing the United States in international competitions, winning at the FIBA Under-19 World Cup (2019), the FIBA Under-17 World Cup (2018), the Youth Olympic Games (2018), and the FIBA Americas Under-16 Championship (2017).

113

> ★ **DID YOU KNOW?** ★
> Hurts qualified for the Texas state powerlifting meet while in high school. As a junior, he squatted 570 pounds, bench-pressed 275 pounds, and dead-lifted 585 pounds.

Who was the first NFL quarterback to rush for at least 10 touchdowns in four consecutive seasons?

When the Philadelphia Eagles selected quarterback Jalen Hurts in the second round of the 2020 NFL Draft, many fans were left scratching their heads. After all, Philadelphia had already signed starting QB Carson Wentz to a four-year, $128 million contract. But Hurts soon made the Eagles look like geniuses, as he took over from Wentz in Week 13 of that season and has never looked back. In his second full season under center, Hurts led Philadelphia to a 14–1 record in games in which he started and a berth in Super Bowl LVII, where he threw for 304 yards and scored three rushing touchdowns, setting the marks for the most rushing yards (70) and rushing touchdowns by a quarterback in Super Bowl history. In 2023, he set career highs for completions, attempts, passing yards, and touchdowns, both through the air (23) and on the ground (15). He rushed for at least 10 scores in his first four seasons as the starter, the first quarterback in history to do so. In 2025, he led the Eagles to victory in Super Bowl LIX and was named the game's MVP.

STAR POWER

4.9 MILLION

Number of followers Maher had on Instagram in 2025.

Who is the most followed active rugby player on social media?

Women's rugby sevens is not the most popular spectator sport in the United States, but **Ilona Maher** is doing what she can to change that. A multisport athlete in Burlington, Vermont, Maher took up rugby in her senior year of high school and was named the nation's top collegiate women's rugby player in 2017 while playing for Quinnipiac University. Maher played for Team USA at the 2020 Summer Olympics in Tokyo and then again at the 2024 Games in Paris, where the team won its first medal ever, a bronze, after a last-second victory over Australia. Off the field, Maher has proved to be a social media sensation, giving her millions of followers on TikTok and Instagram a behind-the-scenes look at the life of an Olympian. She has also been praised as an advocate for body positivity, reminding her fans that champions come in all shapes and sizes.

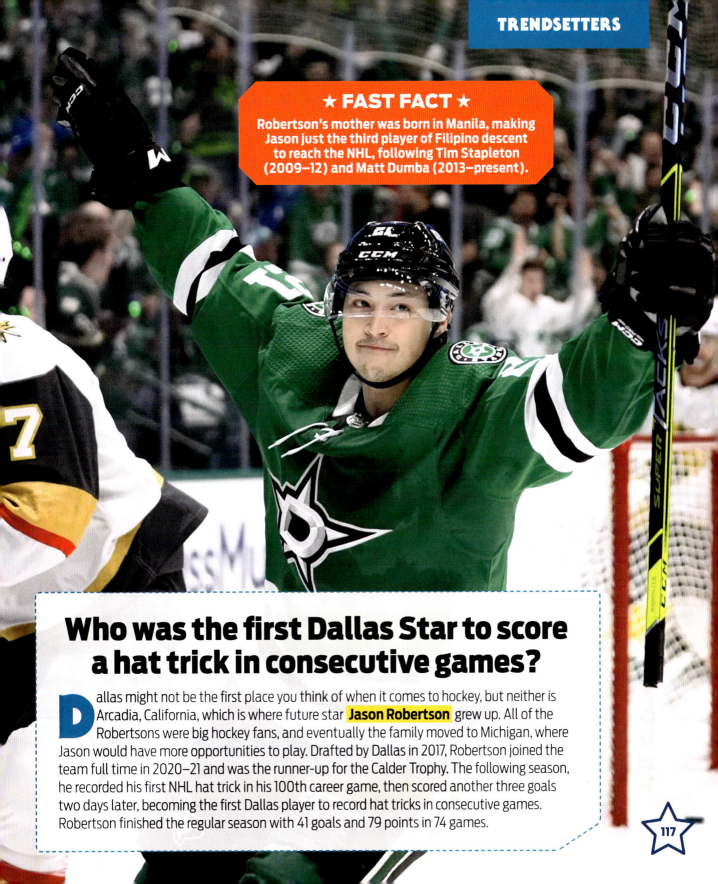

TRENDSETTERS

★ FAST FACT ★
Robertson's mother was born in Manila, making Jason just the third player of Filipino descent to reach the NHL, following Tim Stapleton (2009–12) and Matt Dumba (2013–present).

Who was the first Dallas Star to score a hat trick in consecutive games?

Dallas might not be the first place you think of when it comes to hockey, but neither is Arcadia, California, which is where future star **Jason Robertson** grew up. All of the Robertsons were big hockey fans, and eventually the family moved to Michigan, where Jason would have more opportunities to play. Drafted by Dallas in 2017, Robertson joined the team full time in 2020–21 and was the runner-up for the Calder Trophy. The following season, he recorded his first NHL hat trick in his 100th career game, then scored another three goals two days later, becoming the first Dallas player to record hat tricks in consecutive games. Robertson finished the regular season with 41 goals and 79 points in 74 games.

★ FAST FACT ★
Fox majored on psychology at Harvard University, where he also played hockey and broke the school's single-season record for points by a defenseman (48, in 2018–19).

Which New York defenseman grew up going to Rangers games?

When he was traded from the Carolina Hurricanes to the New York Rangers in 2019, defenseman **Adam Fox** could hardly believe his luck. After all, his father was a Rangers season ticket holder who regularly took his son to see them play at Madison Square Garden. Fox has made the most of playing for his hometown team, finishing the 2019–20 season with eight goals and 34 assists in 70 games, tied for second among all rookie defensemen in goals, and third in points and assists. He turned it up a notch the following season, winning the Norris Trophy to become only the second defenseman in NHL history to win the award before starting his third season. (Boston legend Bobby Orr is the other.) He was also the first Ranger to win the award since Brian Leetch in 1997, leading all NHL defensemen with 42 assists.

TRENDSETTERS

★ FAST FACT ★
Osaka became the first tennis player to light the Olympic cauldron during the opening ceremony at the 2020 Tokyo Olympics.

Who is the first Japanese woman to win a major tennis title?

When she was just three years old, **Naomi Osaka** and her family moved from her native Japan to Long Island, New York. In her WTA Tour debut match as a 16-year-old, she defeated a former U.S. Open champion. Then, in 2018, she beat 23-time Grand Slam singles champion Serena Williams to win the U.S. Open herself, the first Japanese player to claim such a prize. Osaka has since won another U.S. Open and two Australian Opens, and has been ranked the top woman in the world. Osaka has also made an impact off the court, becoming one of the most marketable athletes in the world and an advocate for numerous causes from racial equality to mental health in sports.

119

★ DID YOU KNOW? ★
Lee competed on Season 30 of *Dancing with the Stars*, the seventh Olympic gymnast to be a contestant on the hit show, following Shawn Johnson, Nastia Liukin, Aly Raisman, Laurie Hernandez, Simone Biles, and Mary Lou Retton.

Who is the first Asian woman to win the individual all-around gold medal at the Olympics?

At the 2020 Tokyo Olympics, gymnast Suni Lee admitted she thought she was competing for second place. But when teammate and all-around favorite Simone Biles withdrew, Lee seized the moment and replaced her on floor exercise in the team final. Her performance helped the U.S. win the silver medal. Lee then took the individual all-around, becoming the fifth consecutive American and the first Hmong American to win the gold medal. "My community is so amazing," said Lee. "They were all watching together and got to see me win a gold medal. Many people from the Hmong community don't reach their goals, and I want them to know you can reach your dreams and don't ever give up. You never know."

TRENDSETTERS

Who is the only star to win both the NBA's Most Improved Player and Sportsmanship awards?

The NBA is full of intense competitors who nonetheless appreciate the value of sportsmanship. Few exemplify that better than the Philadelphia 76ers' **Tyrese Maxey**. Drafted with the 21st pick of the 2020 NBA Draft, Maxey began to come into his own in 2021–22 then blossomed in 2022–23, when he averaged 20.3 points per game as the team's second option alongside Joel Embiid. He upped his game even further in 2023–24, averaging career highs in points, rebounds, assists, and minutes played. In recognition, he took home the NBA's Most Improved Player Award. He also won the league's Sportsmanship Award, given to the player who most "exemplifies the ideals of sportsmanship on the court with ethical behavior, fair play, and integrity."

STAR POWER

5.6

Points per game increase in Maxey's scoring average from 2022–23 to 2023–24.

★ **DID YOU KNOW?** ★

Maxey is a huge fan of the Marvel Cinematic Universe. In February 2024, he told SLAM his five favorite Marvel movies were *The Avengers*, *Avengers: Infinity War*, *Black Panther*, *Spider-Man: Far From Home*, and *Iron Man*.

Who was the first defender to be named U.S. Soccer's Female Player of the Year?

The first overall pick of the 2022 NWSL Draft, **Naomi Girma** got her professional soccer career off to an auspicious start. At the end of her first season with the San Diego Wave FC, she was named the league's Rookie of the Year and Defender of the Year, the first rookie to win multiple honors. The following year, she led the Wave to the best regular-season record and was again named Defender of the Year. As a member of the USWNT, Girma has been similarly impactful. After serving as captain of the 2020 CONCACAF Women's U-20 championship team, she joined the senior team and played in the 2023 Women's World Cup. Her outstanding performance that year led to her being named U.S. Soccer's Female Player of the Year, becoming the first true defender to win the award in its history. She was also part of the gold medal winning team at the 2024 Paris Olympics. In 2025, Chelsea signed Girma to a $1.1 million deal, making her the first woman to break the million-dollar mark.

★ **FAST FACT** ★
Born in California to Ethiopian parents, Girma speaks both Amharic and English.

★ **DID YOU KNOW?** ★
In addition to captaining Stanford University to victory in the 2019 Women's College Cup, Girma graduated with a degree in symbolic systems before pursuing her master's degree in management science and engineering.

TRENDSETTERS

Which WWE Superstar competed at the USA Gymnastics Championships in 2016?

Fans of the WWE have quickly taken to **Tiffany Stratton**, thanks in part to her high-flying athletic ability. If you are wondering how she pulls off her finishing maneuver—the Prettiest Moonsault Ever, in which she backflips off the top rope onto her opponent—she might have learned those skills during her years as a competitive gymnast. Stratton, whose real name is Jessica Woynilko, practiced trampoline and tumbling prior to getting in the ring. She even placed third in the Double Mini Trampoline event at the 2016 USA Gymnastics Championships. After joining the WWE in 2021, she has won the NXT Women's Championship, the Women's Money in the Bank briefcase, and the WWE Women's Championship.

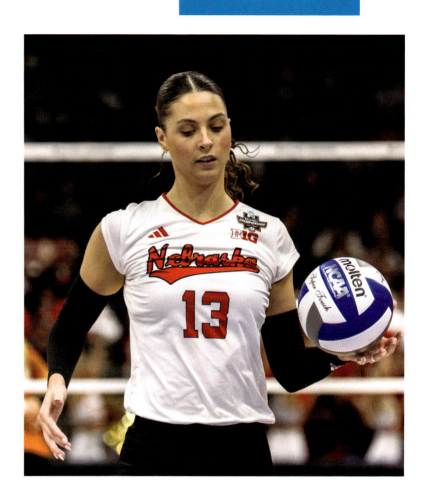

Who was the first pick of the 2024 Pro Volleyball Federation Draft?

After a successful inaugural season, the Pro Volleyball Federation's second draft began with intrigue, as the Indy Ignite traded the first overall pick to the Atlanta Vibe. Minutes later, the Vibe chose opposite hitter **Merritt Beason** from the University of Nebraska. One of the most dominant players in Division I, Beason was named to the AVCA All-America First Team in 2023 and the All-Big Ten First Team in 2023 and 2024. In her final season, she was named senior captain and helped lead her team to a 33–3 record.

Who was the first American skateboarder to win two Olympic medals?

When he was four years old, **Jagger Eaton** got a skateboard as a Christmas gift and began skating almost every day. He earned a sponsorship from Red Bull when he was nine, then entered the X Games at the age of 11, becoming the youngest skater at that time to ever compete. He's only gotten better since, winning a world street title at the Street League Skateboarding Super Crown in 2021 and a world park title at the World Park Skateboarding Championship in 2023; he is the only skater to earn a world title in each discipline. On the Olympic stage, Eaton claimed the bronze medal in street at the 2020 Games in Tokyo, the first time skateboarding was part of the competition, then took silver in street at the 2024 Games.

★ **DID YOU KNOW?** ★

Eaton's parents had their first date at a Rolling Stones concert. Three of his siblings also have names inspired by musicians: Jett, Bowie, and Hendryx.

TRENDSETTERS

★ FAST FACT ★

Eaton was featured in the closing ceremony of the 2024 Olympic Games in Paris. He took the ceremonial flag from track legend Michael Johnson and skated it to the beach where the Red Hot Chili Peppers were about to perform.

125

Player Index

A
Adams, Tyler, 98
Alcaraz, Carlos, 42
Allen, Josh, 60

B
Ball, LaMelo, 107
Banchero, Paolo, 6
Beason, Merritt, 123
Bedard, Connor, 40
Boston, Aliyah, 12
Bowers, Brock, 15
Breakker, Bron, 83
Brink, Cameron, 19
Brown, Sky, 47
Bueckers, Paige, 113

C
Canady, NiJaree, 106
Celebrini, Macklin, 26
Chase, Ja'Marr, 102
Chourio, Jackson, 16
Clark, Caitlin, 67
Crochet, Garrett, 53

D
Dahlin, Rasmus, 59
Daniels, Jayden, 77
De La Cruz, Elly, 38
DeBeer, Anna, 52
Dest, Sergiño, 95
Dončić, Luka, 80
Dunne, Livvy, 97

E
Eaton, Jagger, 124
Edwards, Anthony, 46
Elor, Amit, 14

F
Faber, Brock, 17
Fillier, Sarah, 34
Flagg, Cooper, 24
Fox, Adam, 118
Frech, Ezra, 62

G
Gauff, Coco, 25
Gilgeous-Alexander, Shai, 109
Girma, Naomi, 122
Gu, Eileen, 11

H
Haliburton, Tyrese, 20
Heise, Taylor, 82
Henderson, Gunnar, 84
Herbert, Justin, 70
Holmgren, Chet, 8
Hughes, Jack, 92
Hughes, Luke, 92
Hughes, Quinn, 92
Hunter, Travis, 28
Hurts, Jalen, 114
Hutchinson, Aidan, 18

I
Ionescu, Sabrina, 62

J
Jefferson, Justin, 91
Johnson, Flau'jae, 111

K
Kim, Chloe, 103
Korda, Nelly, 9

Lamb, CeeDee, 21
Lawrence, Trevor, 88
Lee, Suni, 120
Love, Jordan, 95
Lyles, Noah, 71

Maher, Ilona, 116
Makar, Cale, 56
Malinin, Ilia, 100
Marks, Caroline, 39
Matson, Erin, 101
Maxey, Tyrese, 121
McKennie, Weston, 59
McLaughlin-Levrone, Sydney, 99
Merrill, Jackson, 27
Morant, Ja, 73
Morikawa, Collin, 94
Musah, Yunus, 23

Nacua, Puka, 35
Nedoroscik, Stephen, 68
Nix, Bo, 69

O'Neill, Brennan, 43
Osaka, Naomi, 119

Parsons, Micah, 50
Pettersson, Elias, 65
Purdy, Brock, 74

Reese, Angel, 57
Richardson, Sha'Carri, 86
Robertson, Jason, 117
Rodman, Trinity, 37
Rodríguez, Julio, 63
Rodriguez, Lexi, 22

Sinner, Jannik, 75
Skenes, Paul, 45
Skubal, Tarik, 89
Stratton, Tiffany, 123
Stroud, C.J., 17
Swanson, Mallory, 93
Świątek, Iga, 98

Thomas, Gabby, 58
Trew, Arisa, 51

Watkins, JuJu, 48
Watson, Sam, 13
Wembanyama, Victor, 32
Williams, Caleb, 64
Wilson, Sophia, 7
Witt Jr., Bobby, 112

Zumwinkle, Grace, 110

Photo Credits

Front Cover: Erick W. Rasco for Sports Illustrated (Hurts); Brian Rothmuller/Icon Sportswire (Clark); Greg Nelson for Sports Illustrated (Wembanyama); Simon Bruty for Sports Illustrated (Osaka)
Page 6: AP Photo/Matt Kelley
Page 7: Cal Sport Media via AP Images
Page 8: Christian Petersen/Getty Images
Page 9: Michael Reaves/Getty Images
Page 10: Erick W. Rasco for Sports Illustrated
Page 12: Erick W. Rasco for Sports Illustrated
Page 13: AP Photo/Tsvangirayi Mukwazhi
Page 14: AP Photo/Eugene Hoshiko
Page 15: Erick W. Rasco for Sports Illustrated
Page 16: Kiyoshi Mio/Icon Sportswire
Page 17: AP Photo/Matt Krohn (Faber); Patrick Smith/Getty Images (Stroud)
Page 18: Cooper Neill via AP
Page 19: Erick W. Rasco for Sports Illustrated
Page 20: Julien Poupart/Abaca/Sipa USA
Page 21: Perry Knotts via AP
Page 22: AP Photo/Thibault Camus
Page 23: Simon Bruty for Sports Illustrated
Page 24: Ethan Miller/Getty Images
Page 25: Daniel Leal/AFP
Page 26: AP Photo/Eakin Howard
Page 27: AP Photo/Gregory Bull
Page 29: Logan Bowles via AP
Page 33: Greg Nelson for Sports Illustrated
Page 34: Troy Parla/Getty Images
Page 35: Ryan Kang via AP
Page 36: Erick W. Rasco for Sports Illustrated
Page 38: Nick Wosika/Icon Sportswire
Page 39: AP Photo/Gregory Bull
Page 41: Julien Poupart/Abaca/Sipa USA
Page 42: Erick W. Rasco for Sports Illustrated
Page 43: Jeff Moreland/Icon Sportswire
Page 44: Nick Wosika/Icon Sportswire
Page 46: Greg Nelson for Sports Illustrated
Page 47: Simon Bruty for Sports Illustrated
Page 49: John W. McDonough for Sports Illustrated
Page 50: Julien Poupart/Abaca/Sipa USA
Page 51: Anthony Behar/Sipa USA
Page 52: Jamie Schwaberow/NCAA Photos via Getty Images
Page 53: Maddie Malhotra/Boston Red Sox/Getty Images
Page 56: AP Photo/Phelan M. Ebenhack
Page 57: David E. Klutho for Sports Illustrated
Page 58: Tim Clayton/Corbis via Getty Images
Page 59: AP Photo/Jeffrey T. Barnes (Dahlin); Matthew Visinsky/Icon Sportswire via Getty Images (McKennie)
Page 61: Erick W. Rasco for Sports Illustrated
Page 62: AP Photo/Thibault Camus (Frech); Erick W. Rasco for Sports Illustrated (Ionescu)
Page 63: Erick W. Rasco for Sports Illustrated
Page 64: Scott Boehm via AP
Page 65: AP Photo/Rick Scuteri
Page 66: Brian Rothmuller/Icon Sportswire
Page 68: Erick W. Rasco for Sports Illustrated
Page 69: Erick W. Rasco for Sports Illustrated
Page 70: Erick W. Rasco for Sports Illustrated
Page 71: AP Photo/Jeffrey T. Barnes
Page 72: AP Photo/Brandon Dill
Page 74: Erick W. Rasco for Sports Illustrated
Page 75: Erick W. Rasco for Sports Illustrated
Page 76: AP Photo/Chris Szagola
Page 81: AP Photo/Mark J. Terrill
Page 82: M. Anthony Nesmith/Icon Sportswire
Page 83: Faye Sadou/MediaPunch /IPX
Page 85: AP Photo/Thibault Camus
Page 87: Steve Christo/Corbis via Getty Images
Page 88: Greg Nelson for Sports Illustrated
Page 89: David E. Klutho for Sports Illustrated
Page 90: Erick W. Rasco for Sports Illustrated
Page 92: Derek Cain/Getty Images
Page 93: AP Photo/Aurelien Morissard
Page 94: Erick W. Rasco for Sports Illustrated
Page 95: Thomas Lovelock for Sports Illustrated (Dest); Michael Owens via AP (Love)
Page 96: Chris Parent/LSU/University Images via Getty Images
Page 98: Erick W. Rasco for Sports Illustrated (Świątek); Simon Bruty for Sports Illustrated (Adams)
Page 99: Simon Bruty for Sports Illustrated
Page 100: The Yomiuri Shimbun via AP Images
Page 101: Andrew Katsampes/ISI Photos/Getty Images
Page 102: David E. Klutho for Sports Illustrated
Page 103: Ulrik Pedersen/NurPhoto
Page 106: Nathan Giese/Avalanche-Journal/USA TODAY NETWORK via Imagn Images
Page 107: Chris Keane for Sports Illustrated
Page 108: Greg Nelson for Sports Illustrated
Page 110: Nick Wosika/Icon Sportswire
Page 111: Greg Nelson for Sports Illustrated
Page 112: Erick W. Rasco for Sports Illustrated
Page 113: David E. Klutho for Sports Illustrated
Page 115: Erick W. Rasco for Sports Illustrated
Page 116: Julien Poupart/Abaca/Sipa USA
Page 117: AP Photo/Tony Gutierrez
Page 118: Jared Silber/NHLI via Getty Images
Page 119: Simon Bruty for Sports Illustrated
Page 120: Erick W. Rasco for Sports Illustrated
Page 121: Ryan Kang via AP
Page 122: Erick W. Rasco for Sports Illustrated
Page 123: WWE/Getty Images (Stratton); David Buono/Icon Sportswire (Beason)
Page 125: Sean M. Haffey/Getty Images
Back cover: Julien Poupart/Abaca/Sipa USA (Bedard); Nick Wosika/Icon Sportswire (Skenes); Greg Nelson for Sports Illustrated (Edwards); Erick W. Rasco for Sports Illustrated (Gu)